WING

The of the Game

ROWING
The Skills of the Game

ROSIE MAYGLOTHLING

THE CROWOOD PRESS

First published in 1990 by
The Crowood Press Ltd
Ramsbury, Marlborough
Wiltshire SN8 2HR

Paperback edition 1993

This impression 1998

British Library Cataloguing-in-Publication Data

A catalogue record for this book is available from
the British Library

ISBN 1-85223-753-8

Dedicated to my parents Olive and Frank

Acknowledgements

Thanks to all the coaches who have encouraged and supported
me over the last six years. Special thanks to Liz O'Flaherty for
her enthusiasm and patience, to the athletes who were
photographed and to John Shore for all the excellent pictures

Line illustrations by Jan Sparrow

Typeset by Action Typesetting Ltd, Gloucester
Printed and bound in Great Britain by
WBC Book Manufacturers, Bridgend.

Contents

Rosie Mayglothling has represented Great Britain five times, sculling and rowing in a variety of boats. She has coached various crews and was National Coach for the ARA. Rosie has often acted as a technical adviser to various rowing groups, has been a manager for British rowing teams and is now a rowing development officer.

Every Olympic rowing medallist started the sport at a local rowing club without knowing the first thing about the skills needed for top performance. This excellent book will provide a clear, logical and helpful introduction to the sport for anyone who wants to try it. But beware! For rowers are often 'hooked' on the sport very rapidly and you may be too.

Whether your ambition is to enjoy some pleasant relaxation or to join the increasing number of British Olympic medallists, you will find this book invaluable. I am very pleased to be able to give it my support.

DAVID TANNER
Chief Coach UK Men's National Rowing Team

Rosie Mayglothling has been a national coach for six years and before that was herself an international oarswoman. In spite of this she has managed to write a book which avoids the usual coaches' clichés; instead she approaches the technical side of rowing by explaining how the rower's actions will affect the way the boat moves. The result is a book that provides a simple but comprehensive introduction to rowing for the beginner and a useful reminder to the more advanced oarsman of the fundamental principles involved.

CAROL·ANN WOOD
1986 World Silver Medallist, Lightweight Womens Double Scull

Introduction

People have usually viewed the Oxford and Cambridge Boat Race and experienced rowing in a park lake dinghy. Both are rowing and represent the opposite ends of the rowing spectrum in terms of both boat type and training equipment. This book centres around the racing and touring end of the sport and although the principles do apply to other types of rowing craft, the techniques presented are essentially for a sliding seat swivel rowing boat.

This book has been written with the intention of enabling the interested enthusiast to move from a novice level to a proficient standard. The book attempts to familiarise the novice with the equipment, the safety aspects and basic handling skills. Attention is also given to forms of rowing other than racing and information on where to row and how to train has also been included.

While the book is essentially aimed at the beginner, the technical detail will also apply to the experienced oarsman. For many people it has been some time since they learned to row — the early steps are now a blur and the information in this book should remind them exactly what they should be doing.

Rowing is fun and whatever branch of the sport beginners choose to enter, they will enjoy themselves.

1 Background

Fig 1   Start of a fours race.

Great Britain has a long history and tradition of rowing stretching back over the centuries. Documents exist showing that the Roman fleet rowed up the River Thames during the third century to occupy London. Although the earliest use of rowing boats was for military purposes, once the towns became flourishing centres, the commercial implications of rowing boats became very important. The Thames, for example, had very few bridges and had to be crossed by ford or ferry — in the early seventeenth century there were at least 40,000 licensed watermen working on the reaches between Gravesend and Windsor. During the follow- ing centuries their numbers increased and the king, the lord mayor, the City livery companies and rich landowners all had their own barges, while the ordinary citizen hired one of the skiffs which were operated by watermen from the many steps or landing stages up and down both banks of the river. The watermen employed by different companies wore distinctive livery and wagering developed between the gentry on their speed and skill. These watermen's races were the origin of the sport.

One of these wager races still survives today. In 1715 an Irish comedian, Thomas

Doggett, gave a coat and badge to be raced for by six watermen in the first year after completing their apprenticeship. King George I watched the inaugural race and it is said that Handel composed the celebrated *Water Music* for this event. This event has been run annually since that time and is the oldest sporting event in continuous existence. After Thomas Doggett's death in 1721, the race was organised by the Fishmongers' Company who still provide boats and the administrative back up to enable the race to take place. This would appear to have little relevance to today's racing, however, the new ARA Prudential Tracer sculling boat owes a lot to the design of the boats used for the Doggett's Coat and Badge Race.

After these initial races involving the watermen of London, rowing as a sport was taken up by public schools during the nineteenth century. The early races were often discouraged by the schools since they tended to involve rowdy behaviour and a racing crew would think nothing of ramming the opposition or forcing them up the bank. Westminster School and Eton College were two of the early proponents of rowing and soon afterwards the universities of Oxford and Cambridge also took up rowing. The public schools and universities bred a new type of sportsman called the 'gentleman amateur' and with the many professional watermen and artisans a rivalry developed which rumbled on until 1937.

The initial definition of an amateur was very exclusive; not only could he not compete for money or receive any kind of payment for athletic exercise, but the true amateur could not belong to a club containing mechanics or professionals, nor could he be a mechanic or an artisan himself. This meant that the amateurs

Fig 2   The Doggett's coat and badge.

came from a very small group of people such as officers in the armed services, civil servants or members of other 'liberal' professions. However, an interesting association between the amateurs and professionals arose since many of the amateurs used the professionals for advice and coxing in their races. A number of liberally minded oarsmen found that the rule which did not allow a skilled craftsman such as a goldsmith to row because he was a mechanic, but did allow the draper next

Background

Fig3   *The start of the Oxford and Cambridge Boat Race.*

Fig 4   *Henley Royal Regatta, as seen from the church tower.*

Fig 5   A Playboat event.

Fig 6   Steve Redgrave and Andy Holmes, Olympic and World Champions.

door or the unskilled office boy to row, was rather bizarre. It was not until 1956 that rowing became governed by one body, the Amateur Rowing Association (ARA) which stopped this discrimination on basis of job.

Today the ARA still governs rowing in Great Britain and there are over 500 clubs taking part in regattas at different venues and on different types of water all over the country. The international governing body is the Fédération Internationale des Sociétés d'Aviron (FISA) which organises annual World Championships and the Olympic rowing event.

Rowing as a sport, while holding on to its traditional beginnings, is attempting to break out of its élitist mould. The Oxford and Cambridge Boat Race and Henley Royal Regatta are still important events in the rowing calendar, but these two are now surrounded by many other provincial events and even within the high profile races, the mix of rowing people is now considerable. Rowing is a pursuit which is very suitable as a leisure activity, both to explore rivers and to tour, and also purely as a means of exercising. The new breed of funboats enable young people to enjoy themselves and the Proficiency Award Scheme enables youngsters to become more successful by testing themselves against a set standard rather than against other people.

2 Equipment

BOAT VARIETIES

Rowing takes place on rivers, canals, lakes, reservoirs and on the sea. Most major cities in England support at least one rowing club and many schools, universities and businesses also have them. The equipment in the club will reflect the venue and the main emphasis of the club's activities.

Rowing boats can be divided into four broad bands; the first are sleek racing sculls which are narrow and long, the second are touring boats which are designed for carrying people and their equipment, the third are coastal boats which race on the sea and the last are 'starter boats' which are used for introducing novices to the sport.

Rowing and Sculling

Two terms frequently used in conjunction with boat type are rowing and sculling. In rowing, each person has one blade; in sculling they have two. This means that rowing activity is asymmetric with the body twisting slightly to one side. In order for the boat to go in a straight line, the oarsmen on both sides of the boat must have equal power output. In sculling, the activity is symmetrical so people of different abilities may be more easily accommodated in the same boat.

Steering

All boat categories, except for the single and double, have a rudder. In the coxed boat

Fig 7   A single scull.

classes the cox operates the rudder; in the coxless boats a member of the crew steers by moving one of their feet. (this mechanism is further explained in Chapter 7).

The Racing Boat

Fig 10 shows the eight internationally recognised racing boat categories. There are five categories of rowing boat and three sculling boat categories. The boat speed is

Fig 8   A coxless pair.

Fig 9   A double scull.

related to the number of blades, with the sculling boats being marginally slower. Therefore, the quadruple scull is slightly slower than the eight even though they both have eight blades and the double scull is slightly slower than the four even though they both have four blades.

The greater the area of boat in contact with the water, the more resistance there will be, so the racing boat is designed to have as little wetted surface as possible while still maintaining stability and buoyancy. This means that the preferred designs are a pencil shape, but in order to give maximum leverage outriggers are added.

The Coastal Boat

The coastal boat is designed to race on the sea. Although the narrower the craft is, the less resistance it gives to its forward movement, this becomes impractical on the sea – the size of the waves would cause the boat to break up. The coastal boat is much shorter than the racing boat; staggered seating shortens it still further. The coastal four is only 9.2m (30.2ft) compared with 13.25m (43.5ft) for a river coxed four, but there is a move to increase the length of the coastal four to 10m (33ft). This would eliminate the staggered seating and enable the boat to have a far wider use than purely for rowing on the coast. The boat categories in coastal rowing are restricted to fours, singles and pairs.

A safety feature included in the coastal boats is a self-baler. This is opened when the boat is moving along. If a wave swamps the boat it enables the water to drain away through the bottom of the boat.

RACING BOAT TYPES					
Rowing Boats		Name	Rudder	Length (m)	Min. wt. (kg)
	8 +	Eight	Yes	17.00	93
	4 −	Coxless Four	Yes	12.50	50
	4 +	Coxed Four	Yes	13.25	51
	2 −	Coxless Pair	Yes	9.90	27
	2 +	Coxed Pair	Yes	11.15	32
Sculling Boats					
	4 ×	Quad Scull	Yes	13.25	52
	2 ×	Double Scull	No	9.90	26
	1 ×	Single Scull	No	8.00	14

Fig 10   Racing boat types.

Fig 11 A coxed four.

Fig 12 A quadruple scull.

The Touring Boat

The touring boat is designed to carry the rower, together with equipment for a tour. This means the boat must be a little more robust and must have more stability to make moving through locks and other obstacles easier. The ideal touring boat is a cross between a traditional Thames double skiff and a tub pair.

Most touring boats are rigged as sculling boats so that the long stints of work are kept as symmetrical as possible. Additionally, the total navigational width of a sculling boat is only 6m (20ft) as opposed to 7m (23ft) for a rowing boat — rivers and canals that are not normally accessible to a four or an eight can therefore be explored in a double sculling boat.

In Germany there are some touring fours and barges with eight rowing and three coxing. These suit their wide waterways but importing them is an expense that most clubs would not contemplate.

The Starter Boat

There is a variety of equipment available for the beginner. Initially it is better for a novice to learn to scull and then to progress on to a rowing boat. There are two main ARA beginner boats.

The ARA Playboat is designed to encourage watermanship skills in youngsters from age eight upwards. Based on the BAT Canoe design it is a very manoeuvrable boat which is also extremely stable. Its dimensions are:

Length	= 475cm (187in)
Width	= 51cm (20in)
TD	= 137cm (54in)
Scull length	= 255cm (100in)
Overlap	= 17.5cm (6.9in)

The Playboat is very strong and durable and is designed to withstand hard use by youngsters. The rigging specification is in the same ratio as that for a racing sculling boat

Fig 13　A Playboat.

and therefore is directly similar to the adult boats in terms of movement skill.

The ARA Prudential Tracer boat was designed by a consortium who were attempting to produce a stable racing boat. This boat is intended to be an intermediate step between the Playboat and the racing shell. The dimensions are:

Length	= 762cm (300in)
Width	= 37cm (14.6in) (at master section)
Weight	= 18kg (39.7lb) maximum
Depth	= 21cm (8.3in) maximum (inside hull to seat)

There are no restrictions on material, method of construction, fittings, riggers or rigging for the ARA Prudential Tracer boat and drawings of the hull design are available from the ARA. In order to race in Prudential Tracer class events, each boat must be measured and registered with the ARA.

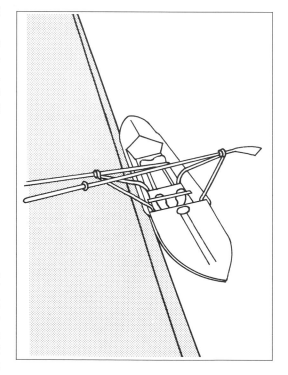

Fig 14　A Playboat.

There are many other stable sculling boats on the market which are worth investigating. They enable the beginner to grasp the sculling action and feel the response of the boat without having to cope with the highly unstable shell of the single sculling boat. Many clubs will also have tub doubles, pairs and fours in which beginners can confidently take their first strokes.

THE PARTS OF THE BOAT

The different parts of the boat have their own technical names. Knowledge of the names and of the location of the different parts is important since by using these terms, for example, 'saxboard', everyone knows exactly which part of the boat is being referred to.

The Saxboard

This is the strengthened area around the top of the boat, just above the waterline. This area has to resist the twisting of the boat and take the stresses and strains applied to the rigger.

The Stretcher

An adjustable bar across the boat on to which clogs or shoes are fitted. The oarsman puts his feet into the shoes and 'jumps off'. As a result, the pressure against the stretcher moves the blade handle and hence the boat.

Fig 15   Stretcher with flexible shoes.

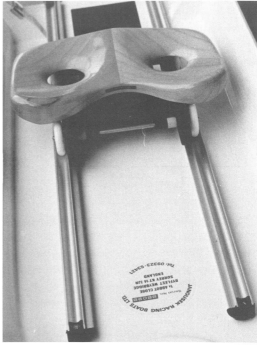

Fig 16   Seat and slide.

Fig 17   Rigger and swivel

The Seat and Slide or Runners

The oarsman takes a longer stroke by using a moving seat. The seat has wheels which enable it to move up and down a slide track. The front and back end of the slide are called the frontstops and backstops respectively.

The Rigger

The rigger effectively makes the boat wider but does so without increasing the wetted surface of the boat. This means that oars can be longer and the leverage of the boat through the water more effective. The rigger supports the pin and swivel — the connection between the blade and boat.

The Swivel

The swivel is plastic and keeps the oar or scull in place. The blade is put in the swivel and is kept securely in place by means of a gate which locks on to the swivel. The pin is the point of contact between the blade and the boat.

The Oar

The oar is an important item of rowing equipment since the leverage of the oar against the boat with the blade in the water provides the movement. The oars are made from wood or carbon fibre, although reinforced plastic is becoming increasingly popular. The oar is divided into three major parts. The handle is the part 'inside' the boat and to which the oarsman applies the power and the loom is the slender shaft which goes into the blade. Only the blade should be in the water and it is by keeping a resistance on the blade that the boat is moved. The blade is roughly rectangular in shape with a curve from top to bottom and from tip to neck. The collar goes around the loom and provides a lip which gives a

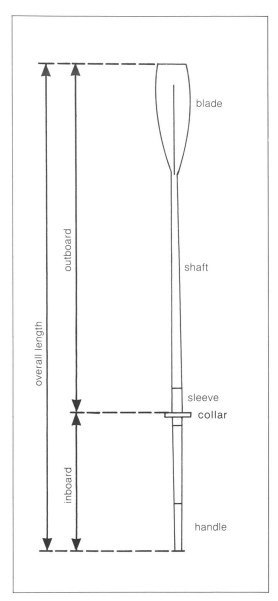

blade

shaft

outboard

overall length

sleeve

collar

inboard

handle

Fig 18   *The parts of the oar.*

Fig 19   *The four oars on the left are composite and the four on the right are wooden.*

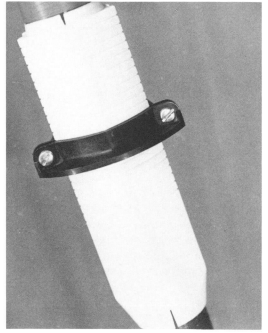

Fig 20   *Oar sleeve and collar.*

constant point of leverage against the pin. The sleeve is plastic and protects the wood in the area under the collar; it can be easily and cheaply replaced — the wooden shaft would, however, present more of a problem.

Fig 21 Oars on racks.

MATERIALS AND CONSTRUCTION

The traditional material used for boat building is wood. Originally boats were clinker built which means that the wooden strips overlapped one another, but this made them both heavy and expensive; nowadays wooden boats tend to have a 'shell' construction. In this method the boat is made up of a thin skin 2mm (0.08in) thick consisting of up to three veneers. The shell may be built around a wooden framework to provide the internal support, or cold moulded and then strengthened.

Increasingly boats are being made from fibre-reinforced plastic (FRP). The most commonly-used fibre is glass, followed by Kevlar, a glass derivative. Strengthening is often provided by carbon fibre which is heat-treated glass and which has a high weight-to-strength ratio. It is used to strengthen the keel and saxboards and enables the total weight of the boat to be reduced while still maintaining the strength of the construction.

FRP boats are moulded; some consist of one layer, whilst others have a sandwich construction. In the latter case, two layers of FRP are separated by a Nomex (nylon) honeycomb which adds to the strength of the construction; these boats can also be put together with either hot or cold cure resins. FRP boats may have traditional strengthening features often provided by wood or by a monocoque design where there is continuous internal bracing.

STORAGE AND CARE OF EQUIPMENT

Whatever the type of boat used, all tend to have high capital costs — a new racing

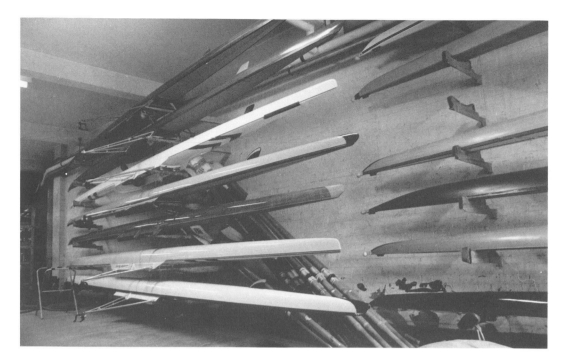

Fig 22   Boat racking for single sculls.

Fig 23   Boat racking for longer boats.

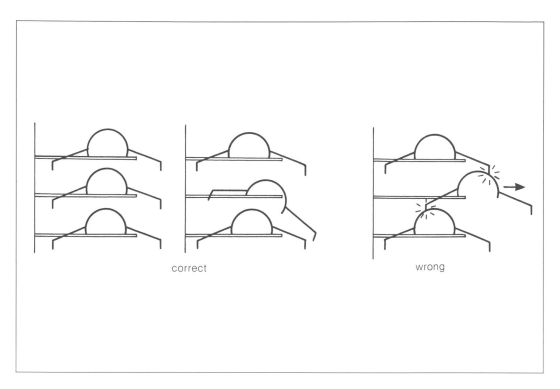

Fig 24   Taking a boat from the rack.

Fig 25   Removing the boat from the rack.

Equipment

Fig 26   Carrying the boat from the boathouse.

eight will cost as much, if not more, than a good-size family car. Even training and touring boats are expensive because of the high labour charge involved in their construction.

As equipment is so expensive it needs a lot of care to ensure as long a life as possible and every oarsman should be aware of this. At the very least, equipment must be cleaned immediately after use; not only does this prevent a build up of dirt and grime, (which will ultimately slow the boat down and make rowing harder) but it also allows for any minor damage to be spotted and repaired before it becomes serious. A quick wash down of the equipment with soapy water does not take long and will considerably lengthen its life.

Care must be taken when moving the boat on land. Before attempting to lift a boat, rowers must always ensure that there are sufficient people involved so that

neither they are hurt nor the equipment damaged. Boats are most often damaged when they are taken from or put back on to the rack or when they are put into or taken out of the water.

Racking in boathouses is usually arranged so that the boat has to be half turned as it comes off or goes on to the rack; care must be taken to ensure the riggers do not puncture the skin or canvas of the boat. When manoeuvring in boat-houses care should be taken especially with the bow, stern, fin and rudder; the cox and coach in particular should watch these areas.

Often it is necessary to place a boat on trestles for cleaning and maintenance. When hard trestles are used they must be positioned in such a way as to support the boat's weight evenly; the overhang at the bow or stern must not be too large. When soft trestles or slings are used, the same

Fig 27 *The oar blade should be carried in front.*

the longer length of the oar will be in vision. It is important when oars are left that they do not get broken or cause damage, in particular leaning them against a wall should be avoided, especially if there is any chance that the wind might blow them over.

CLOTHING

Rowing does not require any special clothing, provided that clothes which do not restrict movements but at the same time which do not flap around, are worn.

In cold weather, wearing lots of thin layers will keep the body warmer than one thick layer and long tops that do not expose the back when rowing are also a good idea. 'All-in-one' suits made of Lycra are becoming increasingly popular amongst rowers; they have eradicated the need for overlapping layers around the midriff and thus enable freer movement. Rowers should note that one third of their body heat can be lost through the head so that in really cold weather a hat is a necessity. A thin, wind-resistant top can also provide useful protection and can keep in body heat.

rule applies, but these should be positioned under the shoulders of the boat. If soft trestles are used to put together a sectional boat, one should be put under the long section and another under the sectional cut. The short section of the boat is then manoeuvred into place and the section bolts tightened while the boat is being held by the crew.

As the oars are so long, care must be taken when carrying them to ensure that they are not damaged and do not cause damage to other people or objects. It is probably best if the oar is carried with the blade in front as this is the most likely part to be damaged and by carrying it this way,

In hot weather rowers must ensure that their neck is covered – wearing a hat may provide the necessary protection. Any cool clothes are acceptable; those with natural fibres provide better insulation against the heat. Rowers should beware of rowing with too few clothes on – sunstroke is a very real possibility when a rower is being cooled by the breeze produced by the boat's forward motion.

3 Safety

The ARA has a very comprehensive *Water Safety Code of Practice*. This should be studied by all rowers and every boathouse should have a copy on display. Rowers should remember to tell someone in the club when they go out rowing — a log book recording everyone's outings is a good system for a club to develop. Emergency numbers should always be clearly displayed in the clubhouse and a first-aid kit should be available at all times.

BUOYANCY

The first concern of anyone getting into a boat is whether or not it will float. Traditionally boats were made of wood which will float even when swamped; this is not true of plastic boats which will sink if holed or damaged. Since there are occasions in rowing when the boat may become swamped, this becomes a major safety factor. This is overcome by providing

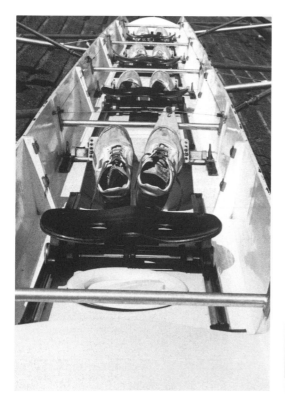

Fig 28 Looking down the boat.

Fig 29 The hatch cover.

buoyancy chambers at the bow and stern of the boat and even under the seating area in some boats. These chambers must be kept in a good state of repair or they will not provide buoyancy. Canvasses must be repaired and the plug, which allows the sections to drain or the air in them to expand when the boat is on the land or in the sun, kept in the boat. The hatch cover or cork must be put in place before the boat goes on to the water.

BOW BALLS *(Fig 30)*

The bow of most boats comes to quite a sharp point and the ARA rules of racing require all boats to carry a bow ball for practice and racing. This must be a solid white ball of rubber or similar material with a diameter of not less than 4cm (1.6in) which is attached to the bow of the boat. Not only does this ball afford some protection to rowers and the boat in the event of a collision, but it also aids in judging races at the finish line.

SHOES

Over recent years there has been a move away from clogs to flexible shoes. Clogs consist of solid wooden soles with a leather upper and a metal heel restraint. The flexible shoes are fitted to the stretcher bar by the upper part, which enables the heel to rise as the rower or sculler moves to front-stops. As a safety feature the shoes must have heel restraints – in the event of the boat sinking or turning over this enables the 'heel raise' to be limited, so the rower can remove the foot from the shoe. Without a heel restraint this is very difficult.

SWIMMING ABILITY

All rowing clubs require the potential member, or parent or guardian of the potential member, to sign a declaration that he is able to swim a minimum of 50m (160ft). This must be taken as the minimum since swimming in cold water with clothes on is very different from swimming in a pool.

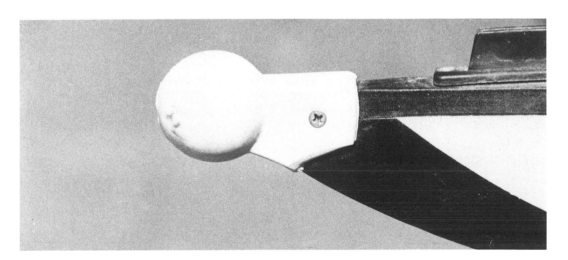

Fig 30   The bow ball

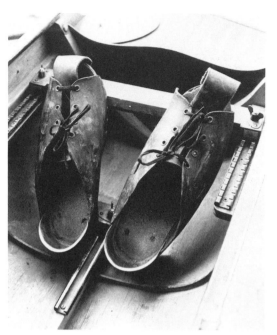

Fig 31   A pair of clogs.

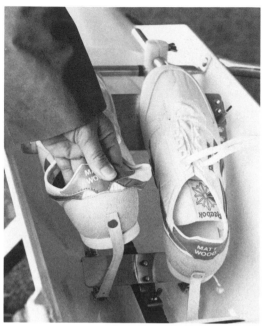

Fig 32   A flexible shoe with heel restraints.

CAPSIZE DRILL
(Figs 33 – 43)

Before rowing on open water it is a good idea for rowers to practise a capsize drill, which will help to reduce the panic that usually accompanies the boat capsizing or sinking. The capsize drill should be carried out automatically so that in the event of a crew or individual sinking a boat, simple procedures can be followed to ensure maximum protection.

The first capsize drill should take place in 'safe' water and preferably in a swimming pool. The first thing to check is swimming ability – a 100m (328ft) swim in rowing kit followed by 50m (160ft) of life-saving leg-kicks is a suitable test. The life-saving leg-kick is economical in effort; it keeps the head clear of the water and the airway straight which makes breathing easier. Another area that should be practised is getting out of the pool without touching the

bottom and without assistance. In an emergency the rower may have to get out of deep water unaided.

CONTROLLED ROLLING PRACTICE

In order to reduce the problems of panic, individuals should try to stay underwater for a few seconds keeping calm. The controlled rolling practice should be carried out in a sculling boat without any sculls. Two people hold the boat clear of the side of the pool and let go. The person in the boat then holds on to the saxboard and rolls the boat over. To give the person confidence in their control they should be encouraged to hold themselves in the seat for three to ten seconds before tapping the bottom of the hull. This should be followed by a controlled surface. Once the person feels competent in this he can put his feet into the clogs and

22

Figs 33 – 43   The capsize drill. In Fig 33, the sculler is pushing the scull
parallel to the boat.

Fig 34   The sculler holds on to the riggers and rolls the boat.

Fig 35   The boat tips over.

Fig 36   The rigger and scull come over.

Fig 37   The boat is almost completely over.

Fig 38   The sculler surfaces beside the boat.

Fig 39   The sculler reaches for the far rigger whilst standing on the
near rigger.

Fig 40   The rigger and scull are half-way over.

Fig 41　The boat is now the right way up.

Fig 42　The sculler moves to the bow of the boat to swim with it to shore.

Fig 43   *The sculler walks the boat ashore.*

repeat the whole practice, ensuring that the knees are kept straight to enable the feet to be removed from the shoes.

Rolling with Blades

The sculls should now be placed in the swivels. The boat should be pushed into the middle of the pool. To roll, the person pushes the scull away until it is parallel with the boat and then rolls to that side. The feet should be taken out of the clogs and the person should complete a controlled surface.

Holding On

Having reached the surface the rower should move towards the bows. It is important that the rower maintains contact

with the boat without putting too much weight on the hull. He should put an arm loosely over the hull and swim, using side-stroke, to the bows.

TURNING THE BOAT

The boat may be towed either upright or the wrong way up. The advantages of turning the boat so it is upright are that it can be towed at a faster speed because of the reduced drag from the riggers and sculls and that the boat takes in less water; the disadvantages of turning the boat are that it wastes time and energy. There is also a possibility of damage or injury to the rower or the boat and more water may be put into the boat by the release of trapped air pockets. However, the increase in

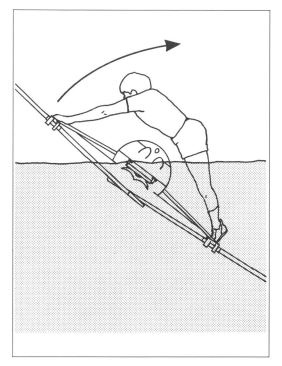

Fig 44   Righting the boat by standing on the rigger.

Fig 45   The boat should be towed into the stream.

resistance when towing the boat upside down is quite considerable and in most cases probably merits turning the boat over.

The boat is turned by standing on the nearside rigger, reaching across the hull to the far rigger and while pushing down with the feet, the boat is pulled over with the arms. This will bring the boat to the upright position.

TOWING THE BOAT

Once the decision to turn the boat has been made then the rower should move towards the bows, maintaining contact with the boat. Once at the bow, life-saving leg-kicks should be used to move the boat. The boat and blades will follow behind the swimmer,

reducing the resistance to the wind and stream. The boat should be towed against the stream or wind towards a landing point. This will ensure that if the boat is drifting towards an obstruction such as rocks or a bridge then it will act as a buffer and the rower's feet, not his head, will hit the obstacle first. In coastal waters and estuaries it may be advisable for rowers to conserve energy and remain with the boat until help arrives.

LANDING THE BOAT

When landing in shallow water, care should be taken to work out speed of drift on to the land and the rower should be aware of the possibility of underwater obstacles.

The rower should ensure that he is on a safe footing and should then walk out to waist depth before doing anything with the boat. If the rower has been in the water for a long time, he should not stand up suddenly but should keep his body as horizontal as possible to ensure there are no sudden changes in blood pressure. The boat is emptied by half turning it, letting the water run out and then gradually lifting one end higher to let more water out. When in deep water, rowers should not attempt to empty the boat but should get out of the water and on to land first.

Fig 46   A coach wearing a buoyancy aid.

Fig 47   A coxless four.

THE EMERGENCY

A capsized boat can still act as a buoyancy aid — it has potentially more flotation than a life-jacket or other aid. Ultimately the person and not the boat is important, and saving the boat should be the last consideration in any action taken.

Life-jackets and Buoyancy Aids

Rowing is difficult while wearing a life-jacket or buoyancy aid. However, coaches in launches and coxes are advised to wear them. At the very least it provides added warmth, and particularly in cold conditions when lots of clothes are worn it may save the life of the cox or coach — swimming in waterlogged clothing is very tiring.

Hypothermia

Hypothermia comes about when the body temperature, which is normally 37°C, drops. Ensure that clothing is warm and suitable for the weather and when touring, rowers must ensure that they have a dry change of kit in the boat. Hypothermia is a condition most likely to be suffered by coxes but every rower should be aware of the symptoms.

Someone with hypothermia is likely to become erratic in behaviour and may start slurring their speech or have difficulty in hearing commands. They may complain of double vision or become very quiet. The situation is potentially very dangerous and instant action should be taken. The person should be wrapped in all available dry kit and even other people's body warmth can be used to raise their temperature. Medical help should be sought as fast as possible.

4 The Sculling and Rowing Strokes

The difference between top rowers and novices is that the former do not waste energy. The total effort put in by both groups is probably not very different, but all the power put in by top rowers moves their boats in the required direction. Understanding a few basic principles will help clarify the action required and will immediately begin to eliminate some of the unnecessary actions often made by rowers. Good performers always make a skill look easy because they waste no energy. Working hard is not enough to make a boat go fast, but if it is combined with sound technique, a winning combination will result.

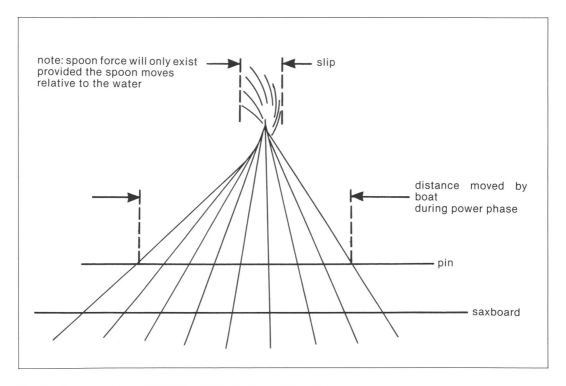

Fig 48   The actual movement of the blade relative to the water.

Boat Propulsion

In order for a rower to be effective in boat propulsion it is important that he understands a few basic principles involved in moving a boat. These are:

1. the blade does not move in the water but the boat is levered past the blade — the acceleration of the handle along with the resistance on the blade causes the pin to move and this in turn causes the boat to move;

2. there is a small amount of 'slip' at the blade end but this helps to keep the pressure on the blade;

3. the boat speed varies through the stroke cycle. Just after the catch the boat is moving at its slowest (*see* Fig 49); as the rower increases the force on the blade handle, the boat speed begins to pick up. In order to maintain the resistance on the blade, the handle must continue to accelerate at an even rate throughout the draw;

4. pressure on the foot stretcher pushes the boat backwards, therefore it is important that the blade is covered (buried in the water) quickly at the catch and an increasing force is applied to the blade handle before the force is applied to the foot stretcher;

5. if blades on each side of the boat are doing different things, the boat will change direction;

6. during the recovery, the body moving up the slide causes the boat to accelerate to the bows thus adding to the speed of the boat.

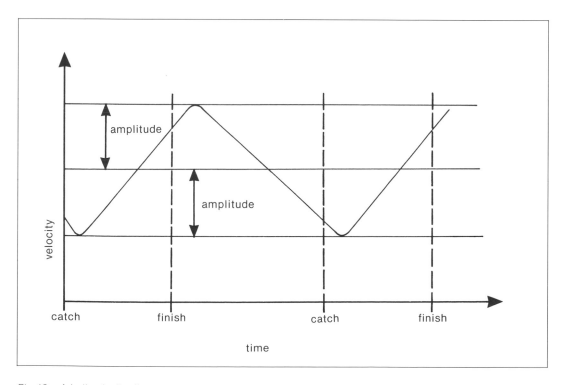

Fig 49 A hull velocity diagram.

The Stroke Cycle

The stroke cycle can be divided into four phases:

1. the catch — the point at which the blade enters the water;
2. the propulsive phase — this is when the blade is in the water;
3. the finish — the point at which the blade leaves the water;
4. the recovery — the blade moving through the air from the finish position to the catch position.

The stroke is a cycle with no beginning and no end and the blade handle never stops during any part of the stroke.

Horizontal Movement

The boat moves horizontally past the blade and so as many vertical actions as possible should be eliminated. The boat should be rowed over the water horizontally and the body movement and the path of the blade handle should also be as horizontal as possible.

The Sculling Cycle
(Figs 50 – 7)

The Catch

1. At the catch the blades should be square and close to the water. The body is rocked over and against the thighs, the

Figs 50 – 57   The sculling cycle. Fig 50 shows the catch — the blades are square and just above the water.

Fig 51 The arms are raised, the blades covered and the knee angle is opening.

Fig 52 The blades are at ninety degrees, the knees are nearly straight and the body is nearly upright.

Fig 53   The sculls just after extraction.

Fig 54   The arms are extended (left hand first) and the body slides on
the recovery.

Fig 55   Just after the catch (back view).

Fig 56   Half-way through the stroke (back view).

Fig 57   Just after the finish (back view).

knees are bent with the shins not beyond vertical and the arms are straight (*see* Fig 50);
2.   the arms are raised to cover the blades and the knee angle begins to open — the movement is horizontal (*see* Fig 51).

The Propulsive Phase

3.   The legs continue to drive and the body begins to open. The handle is still moving horizontally;
4.   when the blades are at right angles to the boat, the legs are nearly straight and the body is nearly upright (*see* Fig 52);
5.   the legs continue to straighten, the body continues to open and the arms then bend.

The Finish

6.   At the extraction, the handles are pushed down and then rolled into the fingers (*see* Fig 53).

The Recovery

7.   The arms are extended with the left hand first. The body rocks over and the knees bend to come to frontstops (*see* Fig 54).

The Rowing Cycle
(Figs 58 – 64)

The Catch

1.   The blade is square and close to the water, the body leans forward against the thighs, the knees are bent with the shins not beyond vertical, the arms are straight and the shoulders are twisted into the rigger (*see* Fig 58).
2.   The arms move upwards to bring the blade down to the water at the catch.

Figs 58−64   The rowing cycle. Fig 58 shows the rowers preparing to take the catch.

Fig 59   The knee angle opens up before the body angle.

Fig 60   The oar is at ninety degrees and the legs are almost straight.

Fig 61   The oar is extracted with the blade kept square.

Fig 62   The hands and body come over before the knees bend.

Fig 63   The shoulders twist around, following the line of the blade (back view).

Fig 64   The shoulders follow the blade handle (back view).

The Propulsive Phase

3.   The knee angle begins to open and the handle begins to move horizontally towards the bows (*see* Fig 59).
4.   The knee angle continues to open and the body begins to lean on the blade handle;
5.   when the blades are at right angles to the boat, the legs are almost straight with the body-weight hanging on to the blade handle (*see* Fig 60).

The Finish

6.   At the finish the legs are straight, the body is leaning backwards, the shoulders are twisted into the rigger and the arms are bent (*see* Fig 61).

The Recovery

7.   The outside hand pushes the handle down and by dropping the inside wrist and rolling the blade into the fingers the blade is made to feather (*see* Fig 62);
8.   The arms straighten, the body rocks over and the knees begin to bend to enable the rower to approach frontstops.

In rowing, the shoulder twist should follow the line of the blade handle.

5   Sculling Progressions

Whenever possible, sculling should be learned before rowing since there are advantages to be gained from single sculling and the individual will soon learn the response of the boat. If one hand is lifted or one leg pushed down harder when sculling, then the response of the boat will be clearly felt and as the actions are all those of the sculler alone, balance will soon be understood since there is no one else to counter these actions.

Watermanship

Watermanship and manoeuvrability are much more easily learned in a single scull. Watermanship is not just about being able to make the boat move but also being aware of how the stream and wind affect the movement and direction of the boat. Watermanship can only really be learned by the person who 'steers' the boat, so often it is only the cox or steersman who learns total control of the boat. Watermanship is important if the oarsman is to become competent and this is best promoted by single sculling.

Once the swimming assessment and capsize drill have been completed, the novice is ready to take to the water.

Carrying the Boat

In the first instance, the beginner will be in a stable boat and since they tend to be heavy, two people will be needed to carry

Fig 65   One person carrying a single scull.

Fig 66   *Carrying a single scull on the head.*

the boat. Some of these boats have carrying handles at both ends to make this easier.

When a certain proficiency is reached and the beginner moves on to a less stable boat, two people may still carry the boat with one holding the bows and the other just behind the stern canvas bulkhead. The sculler with a fine sculling boat may carry the boat by himself; usually this is on the shoulder although some scullers favour carrying the boat on their heads (*see* Fig 66).

Launching the Boat

The gate which will be on the waterside when the boat is in the water should be undone before putting the boat in the water. The boat is then lowered into the water with the bows facing upstream, as manoeuvr-

ability is better when rowing against the stream.

Getting In *(Figs 67 – 72)*

Once the boat is in the water then the nearside scull should be put into the swivel (*see* Fig 67). There are both bowside and strokeside sculls. The bowside scull has either green tape or the letter 'B' on it and the strokeside scull has either red tape or the letter 'S' on it. When sitting in the boat, the bowside is on the left and the strokeside is on the right. Once the bankside scull is in, the waterside scull should be placed in the swivel (*see* Fig 68).

When the sculls are in place the seat is moved half-way along the slide. The ends of the scull handles are placed together and held in the waterside hand. Putting the ends

Fig 67 – 72   *Getting in. Fig 67 shows the nearside scull being placed into the swivel.*

Fig 68   The waterside scull is placed in
the swivel.

Fig 69   The scull handles are brought
together to provide stability.

Fig 70   The sculler sits down.

Fig 71   The outside gate is shut.

Fig 72   The sculler pushes off from the landing stage.

of the sculls together makes the boat reasonably stable and gives the sculler room to move around in the boat. The bankside hand holds on to the bankside rigger. The waterside foot is then placed on the cross-bracing at frontstops and the weight transferred from the back leg and hand on to the leg in the boat. The bankside leg is then brought into the boat and placed in the shoe or clog; at the same time the sculler sits down on the seat. Using the bankside hand, the sculler pushes out from the bank and leans out to do up the waterside gate, still keeping the blade handles together.

Adjustments in the Boat

Most boats are built so that different people can use them and there are various adjustments that can be made. In the early stages the only adjustment necessary will be to the foot stretcher. To position this correctly the sculler should sit with legs straight and with the sculls pulled into the body. When the body is leaning slightly back the sculls should be held apart at a width of one-and-a-half hands (*see* Fig 74) and the thumbs, which are on the ends of the sculls, should just touch the body. The stretcher should be adjusted to move to this position at the finish phase of the stroke cycle.

The Safe Position
(Fig 75)

The hands should hold the ends of the sculls lightly and the thumbs should be placed over the ends of the sculls as

Fig 73   The stretcher should be moved to allow one-and-a-half hand's width between the ends of the sculls.

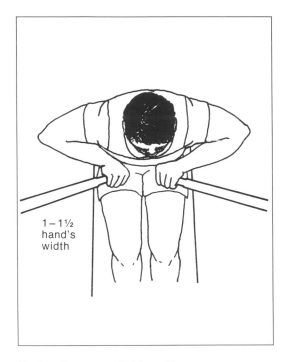

1 – 1½ hand's width

Fig 74 The correct finish position.

mentioned above. The scull handles will overlap in the boat so that the left hand is always nearest the stern of the boat. The safe position is when the legs are flat with the sculls held in each hand and the arms out straight. The blades should be at about ninety degrees to the boat and flat on the water.

This is called the safe position because the boat can be rocked from side to side, but providing that the hands are kept together, there will be very little sideways movement.

Confidence Drills

A good idea in order to gain confidence is for the rower to start by finding out how stable the boat is. For this a few basic rules should be followed. The blade handle

Fig 75 The safe position.

Figs 76 and 77   *Rocking the boat by raising and lowering the hands.*

Fig 77

49

Figs 78 and 79   The scull handles are pushed down in the boat which is
rocked from side to side.

Fig 79

should not drift past the side of the body and in most cases the sculler should hold on to the scull handles:

1. the sculler starts in the safe position. The blades are left on the water and the hands moved up and down — the boat will rock from side to side (*see* Figs 76 and 77);
2. the sculler starts in the safe position, holds both sculls in one hand and puts the other hand behind his back. He then changes hands, gradually increasing the speed of the exercise;
3. the sculler rocks the boat by pushing down alternately with his heels. The hands should be kept off the blade handles which should be positioned over the thighs;
4. the sculler lifts one blade off the water surface. Keeping both handles pushed down in the boat the sculler rocks the boat from side to side and slaps the blades on the water (*see* Figs 78 and 79);
5. the sculler balances with both blades off the water and sees how long he can hold this position. Outward pressure is used on the blades and the heels are pressed down to maintain balance;
6. the sculler stands up on frontstops holding the ends of both sculls in one hand, keeping the scull blades on the water. He rocks the boat from side to side (*see* Figs 80 – 82).

There are many more confidence drills, some of which are easy, and others, such as headstands on frontstops which require reasonable gymnastic skill. When learning in a group each member may set a different confidence drill for the others in the group.

Manoeuvres

Once confidence has been gained the next step is to learn how to manoeuvre the boat. The sculler starts by using one scull only

Figs 80 – 82   Standing on frontstops and rocking the boat from side to side.

Fig 81

Fig 82

52

Figs 83 and 84   *One scull is kept flat on the water whilst the other is used to turn the boat.*

Fig 84

Fig 85   Paddling − spin turning the boat, paddling on with the left hand and backing with the right hand.

Fig 86   Paddling − the left hand is nearer the stern.

Fig 87   Arms-only paddling.

and brings the other scull in towards the ribs with the blade flat on the water for safety reasons. The blade being used should be held square and dropped in the water while the handle is moved towards the body. The sculler pushes down with his hand and as the blade comes out of the water and recovers, the procedure is repeated. If this action is continued then the boat will turn in a complete circle (*see* Figs 83 and 84). This manoeuvre can then be tried using the other hand. It may also be repeated when the blade is in the water and the hand pushed away from the body — this will turn the boat backwards. A quicker turn may be produced if the sculls are used alternately with one side pushing forwards and the other backwards (*see* Fig 85).

Many beginners find terms describing the direction of movement very confusing. The terms 'backwards' and 'forwards' refer to the direction of movement of the bows and not the direction the sculler faces. Therefore 'forwards' is when the bows lead the way and 'backwards' is when the stern leads the way with the bows following.

Paddling and Sliding

Paddling is when both hands are used together to move the boat in a straight line. At first only the arms should be used while ensuring that the left scull remains nearer the stern. This action can be reversed to move the boat backwards in a straight line.

Once the sculler has become proficient in moving the boat in a straight line, then the slide should be practised (*see* Figs 88 – 93). The sculler should still keep the blades square at all times with the left hand nearest the stern. During the recovery sequence the arms are straight and the body bent over as the sculler moves up the slide. During the propulsive phase when the blades are in the water, the legs drive first, the body moves and finally the arms bend.

Fig 88   One-quarter-slide paddling.

Fig 89   Half-slide paddling.

56

Figs 90 – 93 Sliding. Fig 90 shows the sculls, which are square at the catch.

Fig 91 The sculls are square at the finish.

Fig 92   The sculls are square after the extraction.

Fig 93   The sculls are square during the recovery.

The cycle should then be repeated. The sculler should gradually introduce the slide during the recovery with an emphasis on the hands – body – slide sequence, with the left hand leading.

Stopping the Boat
(Figs 94 and 95)

Once able to move the boat, the sculler should also learn how to stop it. The safe position is the starting point and from here, the blades should be lifted and slapped on the water. Next they should be slapped on the water and buried and finally slapped on the water, buried and turned by dropping the wrists. The sequence is slap – bury – turn. The sequence should be practised while paddling forwards and the boat speed then progressively increased until a full

emergency stop can be undertaken safely and effectively. Variations on the emergency stop are when the boat is rowed backwards or when only the blade on one side is put in the water, thus causing the boat to turn.

Feathering

Feathering should only be introduced once the sculler can paddle continuously for ten to fifteen minutes. Being taught to feather the blade too early in the learning process causes many bad habits.

The blade is feathered by rolling it into the fingers. The thumbs control the action and the wrists should remain flat (*see* Fig 96). This action should initially be practised in a stationary situation and then incorporated into the sculling sequence. Two

Figs 94 and 95   Stopping the boat. In Fig 94 the sculls are being slapped on the water.

6 Rowing Progressions

By its very nature, rowing requires at least two people in the boat. Immediately this means that the rower not only has to co-ordinate and time his own movements, but synchronise them with at least one other person.

First Strokes

As rowing relies on other people, it is often safer for the rowers involved to take their first strokes in a bank tub, a rowing tank or when the boat is held against the land. The bank tub is a floating box with the inside of the box fitted out in the same way as a boat. The tub is flat bottomed, very stable and tethered to the bank to prevent any forward or backward movement. The action and feel are the same as when in a boat. However, one major difference is that when the blade moves through the water, the tub stays still. A rowing tank is very similar to a boat but is constructed in concrete in a pool. The rowing action causes the water to move around in the pool rather than creating any forward movement (*see* Fig 99).

Carrying the Boat

To carry a rowing boat, rowers usually stand opposite their rigger and hold the

Fig 98 Getting waterborne.

Fig 99   A rowing tank.

Fig 100   The boat being carried at shoulder level.

boat upside-down by the saxboard at waist level. Sometimes it is necessary to hold the boat higher — usually at shoulder level; certain conditions may make it essential to hold the boat very high and this can be achieved by standing under the boat and holding it over the head by both saxboards.

When turning the boat over, it should be ensured that sufficient people are present to carry out the operation safely. Everyone should know which way the boat is to be turned (which set of riggers is coming up and over) and everyone must work together on the command. Handholds inside the boat should be strong and secure; boats must not be held by the stretchers or by the cross-bracing of the slide runners. When the boat is turned over, those who have to move should duck under the boat, preferably one at a time. When all the crew is on one side of the boat, they must ensure that it is being lifted and carried and not rested on thighs or knees.

When putting a boat into or lifting a boat out of the water, each crew member should put one hand on the outside of the hull to ensure that the boat is kept clear of the landing stage. In particular, care should be taken so that the fin and rudder are not damaged and the outside riggers kept clear of the water.

Launching the Boat

The boat is launched with the bows pointing upstream. The oars should already have been carried down to the water's edge. The cox or a designated member of the crew holds on to the boat while the oars are brought to the boat.

Figs 101–105   *Putting the boat on the water. The boat may be turned by 'throwing' it over the head.*

Fig 102   Guiding the boat down.

Fig 103   The boat is held inside by a secure part of the structure.

Fig 104   The boat is 'walked' to the water's edge.

Fig 105   One hand is used to protect the hull from the landing stage.

Getting In *(Figs 106 – 11)*

Rowing in a crew necessitates discipline and either the cox or, in a coxless boat, the steersman must give orders to ensure everyone carries out their tasks simultaneously. The bankside members of crew must put their oars in the swivels and hold on to the boat before the waterside crew members climb in or the boat may roll over. A little discipline with someone in command ensuring that the correct procedures are followed will easily overcome this.

The bankside oars are placed in the gates and rowers getting in stand on the bowside of the rigger. Each crew member rowing with blades on the waterside should slide his blade across the boat and put one hand on either side of the saxboard. The waterside foot is put on frontstops and his weight lowered on to the seat while the bankside foot is put straight in to the shoe or clog. Once in the boat the first thing the crew member should do is to put the oar in the swivel, close the gate securely and place the blade flat on the water with the button (collar) pressed out against the pin. Once the waterside crew members have put their oars in the swivels, bankside crew members should follow the same procedure for getting into the boat. Everyone then pushes off with his bankside hand.

Adjustments in the Boat

The stretcher position should be adjusted to the finish phase of the stroke cycle. The rower sits at backstops with legs straight, leaning slightly backwards with the blade held close to the body. The shoulders should be twisted in line with the handle. The end of the oar handle should be in line with the side of the body (*see* Fig 113). If the handle sticks out too far, the stretcher

Figs 106 – 11   Getting in. The waterside oars are not put in until the bankside oars are in the swivels.

Fig 107 *The waterside rowers move their blades across and put one foot in the boat.*

Fig 108 *The swivel is undone and the gate opened.*

Fig 109   The oar is placed in the swivel.

Fig 110   The gate is secured.

Fig 111 The bankside rowers put one foot on frontstops and push off from the landing stage.

Fig 112 Bankside rowers pushing off from a beach.

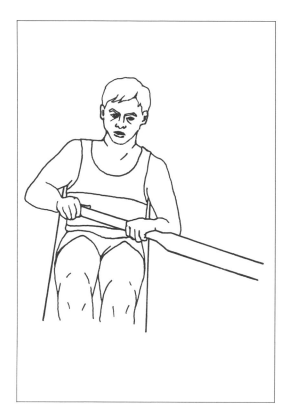

Fig 113 The end of the oar handle should be in line with the side of the body.

should be moved towards the bows and if there is not enough handle in front of the body, the stretcher should be moved towards the stern.

Once everyone in the crew has adjusted their position correctly and is ready to start rowing, the crew 'numbers off' from the bows. So each crew member is given a number: Bow, 2, 3, 4 and so on. The crew members should only number off when they are ready to start rowing.

When rowing commences, crew members must ensure that their hands are positioned on the blade so that there is a gap of roughly the width of two hands between them and with the outside hand at the end of the oar handle. Wrists should be flat when the blade is square and the thumbs positioned under the handle.

Rowing Positions

Rowing with others requires everyone to understand the different positions assumed during rowing. The correct postures should be adopted by each rower.

Backstops (Fig 114)

1. Legs straight, body sits back past the vertical, oar handle touching the ribs and oar feathered off the water.

Hands Away (Fig 115)

2. Legs straight, body back past the vertical, arms straight and oar feathered off the water.

Recovery (Figs 116 and 117)

3. Legs straight, body swung over, arms straight and oar feathered off the water.

Half-Slide (Fig 118)

4. Legs partially bent, body swung over, arms straight and oar square just off the water.

Frontstops (Fig 119)

5. Legs fully compressed, body swung over, arms straight and oar square just off the water.

The Safe Position

The safe position in rowing is with the legs straight, the body upright and the arms straight. The blade should be flat on the water and each crew member should have his hands held at the same height. From this position the balance of the boat can be

Fig 114   Backstops.

Fig 115   Hands away — arms-only rowing.

Figs 116 and 117   Recovery. The arms and body come over.

Fig 117   Rowers holding the recovery position with the hands and body
over the legs.

Fig 118   Half-slide.

Fig 119   Frontstops.

checked if rowers on the two sides raise and lower the handles alternately. If in a reasonably stable boat, the crew may sit in the recovery position and apply pressure alternately with each foot: the boat will rock from side to side. Another balance skill can be completed in the recovery position if crew members on each side alternately push out on the pins with the buttons; again the boat will rock from side to side. Equal outward pressure on the pin is very important for the balance and stability of the boat. Using the inside hand only is also a good exercise (*see* Fig 120).

Paddling and Sliding

This should be undertaken in pairs and should be from the backstops position with fixed seats and square blades. If a four is being used then two people should paddle

while the other two balance the boat, maintaining the safe position.

Gradually the body swing may be introduced and then the slide until, in pairs, the crew can row full slide strokes, while maintaining square blades. It is important that a smooth, continuous action is developed and that the crew extract blades together.

Once the crew have experienced rowing in pairs then they should return to fixed seats with square blades with the whole crew so that the stroke can gradually be built up with all the rowers.

Stopping the Boat

As rowers always face in the opposite direction to that of boat movement, emergency stops occasionally become a necessity. These should be practised in the early stages of rowing.

Fig 120   Rowing using the inside hand only.

To start, the boat should be stationary and the crew members in the safe position. In pairs, the blades are slapped flat on the water. Then the blades are slapped and buried and finally progress is made to slapping, burying and turning the blade by dropping the wrists. This slap, bury and turn procedure should then be practised whilst the boat is moving. It should also initially be done in pairs with other crew members sitting still in the boat, starting with fixed seat paddling and gradually bringing in the slide. Once all the crew members feel competent to perform the emergency stop in pairs, then the whole exercise may be repeated with the whole crew taking part, starting from fixed-seat rowing, and again gradually progressing on to the slide.

Paddling Backwards

In order to paddle backwards, the rower turns the blade over so that the concave side is facing the bows. The rower sits in the backstops position and by straightening the arms with the blade in the water, the boat is moved backwards. During the recovery phase, the blade should be turned flat and skimmed over the surface of the water. Once this action has been successfully completed then the body swing and eventually the slide can also be added. An emergency stop while rowing backwards should also be practised.

Turning

In a crew boat, manoeuvring and turning require more co-ordination than in a single boat. Turning the single allows the sculler to concentrate on one scull; in rowing it requires the different sides of the boat to complete different tasks.

Strokeside crew members should sit still in the boat while bowside members paddle backwards for three strokes. Strokeside members then paddle three strokes forward while bowside members sit still in the boat. This should be repeated until the boat has been turned in a complete circle; the boat should then be turned in the other direction. Once the crew becomes more proficient, the slide may be used. In this case strokeside crew members 'pull on' while bowside members recover on the water and then bowside crew members 'back down' whilst strokeside members recover on the water. The spin turn will rotate the boat in quite a small area.

Feathering

Feathering in rowing, as in sculling, should not be attempted until all the rowers are fully competent at the rowing stroke. In rowing it is the outside hand which taps the handle down to bring the blade out of the water and the inside hand which turns the blade on to the feather.

A common fault among beginners is excessive gripping of the handle. Although it is the inside hand which turns the blade on to the feather, the shape of the loom at the gate is such that the blade will 'fall' in that direction once it starts to go on to the feather. This means that the hands only control the oar and do not need to grip the handle; the outside wrist should remain flat at all times so that the handle spins in this hand.

Landing

The method for landing the boat is the exact opposite to that of launching it, and the order for disembarkation, together with the carrying and racking of the boat should just follow this method in reverse.

7 Coxing, Steering and Watermanship

Although this chapter is primarily about coxing and steering, it would be wrong to assume that it is only relevant to coxes as many boats are coxless.

The cox may steer two types of boat. The most common is the stern-steered boat, and in this case the cox sits facing the rowers and is the nearest person to the stern of the boat (*see* Fig 122). The other type of coxed boat is called the front-loader – in this boat, the cox lies half under the bow canvas with his or her back to the crew (*see* Fig 123). The two positions distribute the cox's weight in a slightly different manner and in small boats such as pairs, or even in some fours, it is considered that the weight is better placed in the bows with the crew nearer the stern – hence these boats are often bow-steered.

THE ROLE OF THE COX

The cox is in charge of the boat and its crew and is a part of the crew. The first duty of the cox is to ensure the safety of the crew and other water users and to look after the equipment the crew is using. Whilst on the water, the cox must ensure that everything is made as easy as possible for the crew. As the steersman of the boat, the cox is likely to be held legally responsible for any

Fig 121   Coxing and steering.

Fig 122   A stern-steered boat; the cox has a *speaker system*.

Fig 123   A front-loader — the cox steers from the bow.

damage or injury caused by their boat.

An essential requirement for every cox is that he is able to swim, and the same swimming test as undertaken in the capsize drill (*see* page 22) should be given to the cox. It is a good idea if a cox also undertakes sculling and rowing lessons, particularly in the early stages, if he is to have a real understanding of how a rowing boat behaves. Common sense is an essential ingredient for every cox along with a cool-headed approach to dealing with situations as they develop and the self confidence to act effectively. Added to this, a cox must have the ability to judge speed and distance and have a good memory. The duties of a cox include the organisation of the crew both on and off the water and so his voice is a very important asset and control and projection may need to be taught – the voice should come from the diaphragm and not from the throat.

WEIGHT

There are minimum weight requirements for coxswains: under ARA rules, the minimum weight for women and juniors is 40kg (88lb) and for men it is 50kg (110lb). Under FISA rules the minimum weight for women is 45kg (99lb). There are, however, coxswains who have been over this weight yet who have made a significant contribution to the crew – lightness is not everything and carrying an experienced but heavier cox may produce a better result.

GENDER

When racing at regattas in Britain, the sex of the cox does not have to be the same as that of the crew and in many events women cox male crews since they are often lighter than men. In international races, the sex of the cox is the same as the sex of the crew.

SAFETY AND PROTECTION

The problem of hypothermia has already been mentioned (*see* Chapter 3) but it is worth emphasising how important it is that a cox wears appropriate clothing for the prevailing weather conditions. In wet or windy weather, body heat can be lost very quickly through clothing unless the top layer is windproof. Lots of thin layers are far more effective than one thick layer as air trapped between the layers acts as insulation. Wellington boots should not be worn in the boat – in the event of a capsize or sinking they are very dangerous as they are very heavy when filled with water.

Not all cox's seats are very comfortable and it may be necessary for the cox to take some sort of padding to ensure comfort throughout the duration of the outing. Another safety factor which should be considered is when dead weight has to be carried if either the cox or boat do not weigh enough. If this is the case, then the weights should on no account be attached to the cox. Similarly, any amplification equipment should be in the boat and not attached to the cox.

The cox should wear a life-jacket when on the water as the layers of clothing being worn will quickly impair swimming ability. Caution should be exercised by the cox when in a front-loader boat especially as it is not recommended that a life-jacket is worn – if the boat capsizes, a life-jacket could prevent the cox from leaving the boat.

DUTIES OF THE COX

Before an outing, the cox must ensure that he has a sound knowledge of local water conditions, together with the club rules. The cox is expected to know all the commands and procedures relevant to the outing, and once the crew becomes proficient he or she should also know the content of the outing and be able to instruct the crew to carry this through. The cox is responsible for the maintenance of the steering equipment to ensure that it remains in good working order, the general working condition of the boat and such things as the greasing of oars.

GOING AFLOAT

The oars should be carried to the launching site before the boat. Once the crew are reassembled around the boat, the cox should ensure that everyone is standing in the correct position in order to lift the boat clear of the rack. Each crew member should stand opposite their rigger in order to carry the boat and any commands must be given by the cox who is responsible for the boat. The cox should follow the boat out of the boathouse in order to ensure that neither the riggers nor any other equipment causes damage to the boat. The cox also gives the commands to turn the boat once at the launch site and ensures that the boat is put safely on the water.

GETTING WATERBORNE

The boat should be put on to the water with the bows facing upstream. The cox should pay particular attention to any local obstacles which may cause damage to the boat, particularly to the fin or rudder, when the boat is being put on the water. Once the boat is on the water the cox holds it (usually somewhere in the middle to ensure control) while the crew fetch their oars. The boating procedure and the order of embarkation should be followed as described in Chapter 6. Once the crew is in the boat, the cox must decide whether to adjust the equipment at the landing stage or on the water. The cox is the last person to get into the boat and normally pushes away from the landing stage.

POSITION AND POSTURE IN THE BOAT

Whether in the stern or on a front-loader, the cox should move as little as possible. Any unnecessary movement can upset the balance of the boat and in particular the cox should not lean out of the boat to look ahead. His body should be braced to prevent any backwards and forwards movement, but should stay relaxed. The rudder lines must be kept taut to prevent the rudder from flapping around and so that sensitivity and response to movement remains constant.

DURING THE OUTING

The cox is in control of the boat and, as part of the crew, should be coached, but in any potentially dangerous situation the cox must take control and override all other instructions. The crew must obey the cox's orders. Once the boat is moving, the cox has the responsibility to steer as efficiently and effectively as possible — this means applying the rudder little and often. The cox's instructions must be clear and concise and if using an amplification system he must be clear on how to operate it.

AFTER THE OUTING

When returning to the landing site, the cox must ensure that the boat is travelling against the stream in order to have maximum steering with minimum speed. Either the cox or bowman should get out of the boat first, depending on the landing site and wind and stream conditions. The landing directions are the reverse of launching and are clearly described in Chapter 6. Before the boat is put on to the rack it should be cleaned and checked for any damage – again this is one of the roles of the cox.

Fig 124   A stern-post rudder.

COMMUNICATION

For a cox to be very effective in the boat it is necessary that he is aware of the feel of the boat and can therefore help the crew row more efficiently. Initially this may be quite difficult, but provided the cox learns to communicate with the coach and the crew early on, he will be able to relate the feel of the boat to particular problems within the crew. The best coxes are often good coaches and many have progressed to become very successful international coaches.

STEERING
How the Rudder Works

The rudder is attached to a bar and from this bar two rudder lines feed into the cox's area. In a stern-steered boat, the rudder lines are not crossed (*see* Fig 124) and the cox pushes one hand forward in the direction in which he wishes the boat to move. To turn to bowside the cox pushes his right hand forward – this causes the right side of the rudder bar to turn, the movement of the rudder causes the stern to slide to strokeside and the realigned boat travels towards bowside. In a front-loader or when an oarsman is steering by foot, the rudder lines are usually crossed. This enables the oarsman to point his toe in the direction in which he wishes to move, or enables the cox to point the steering lever in the direction in which he wishes to travel.

When the rudder is applied, water piles up against its forward face (*see* Fig 126). This acts as a brake and pushes the stern of the boat around (*see* Fig 127). The action of the rudder has little effect on the bows –

Fig 125   The rudder when straight.

Fig 126   The rudder is being applied —
this causes the water to pile up against the
side of it.

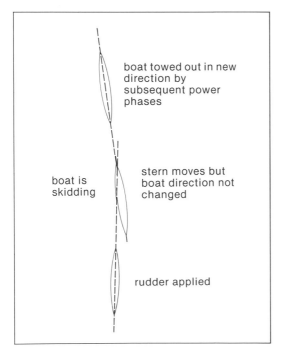

boat towed out in new
direction by
subsequent power
phases

boat is
skidding

stern moves but
boat direction not
changed

rudder applied

Fig 127   The boat skids when the rudder
is applied.

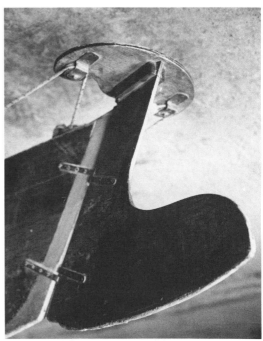

Fig 128   The bigger the rudder, the more
efficient it is for turning.

this results in the apparent time delay before the boat reacts. The longer the boat, the longer this delay appears so the eight seems to turn more slowly than a pair.

When to Steer

The art of good steering is not to upset the rhythm. Use of the rudder will cause the boat to roll to the outside of the turn, for example, turning left will roll the boat to the right. If the rudder is applied when the blades are out of the water, it acts efficiently but will upset the balance. On the other hand, if the rudder is applied when the blades are in the water, it is less efficient but will not upset the balance to such a great extent.

The most efficient rudder for turning a boat would be one that is very large; however, the use of such a rudder would cause more drag and would seriously upset the balance of the boat. Increasingly the tendency is for small flag or teardrop rudders (*see* Fig 129) to be used either at the stern or on the fin. In order to minimise any upset to the rhythm and balance of the crew, the rudder should only be used when the blades are in the water. This requires the cox to anticipate any manoeuvres that need to be made — a good cox will warn the crew that the rudder is about to be used so that they can compensate for the balance upset by adjusting their hand heights.

Small rudders have to be applied more often than large rudders with the rudder at the stern of the boat being the most efficient. In racing boats, the aim is to keep the boat in as straight a line as possible and to minimise the drag — the rudders in these boats therefore tend to be sited behind the fin and are very small.

Steering Hints

Emphasis should be placed on using the rudder as little as possible. The rudder should be applied at the catch and straightened at the finish of the stroke. This means that if the boat is to go around a bend, the rudder should be applied in a series of 'squeezes', with the rudder kept straight when the blades are out of the water. The cox should anticipate the

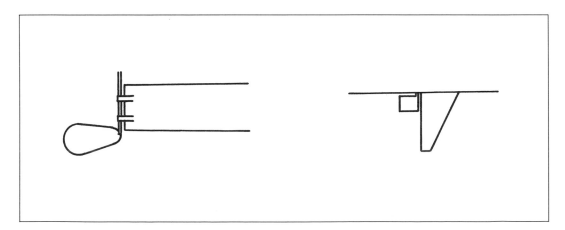

Fig 129 A large stern rudder (left) and a small flag rudder behind a fin (right).

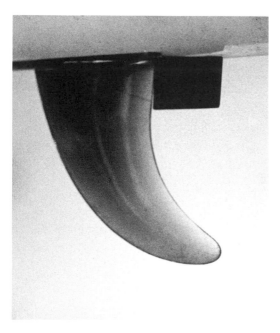

Fig 130   A fin and rudder.

steering so that the rudder is used little and often rather than late and continuously. The bows of the boat should be lined up on distant objects so that corrections are kept to a minimum. The boat will roll to the outside of the turn and if the turn is sharp then the cox should warn the crew to enable them to compensate for the loss of balance.

Basic Commands

Commands to the crew should be both concise and consistent. If necessary the commands should be aimed at individuals or the crew as a whole in order to concentrate their attention on the task in hand. The commands must be understood and heard by every member of the crew. For a novice cox, steering is the most important part of his role and commands rather than advice or coaching are

necessary. The safe transport of the boat and crew is the prime concern of the cox.

Steering in Particular Situations

The Steering Foot (Fig 131)

Many boats are steered by a rower with the rudder line which is attached to a special plate on a steering shoe. This shoe swivels, causing the rudder lines to be pulled to strokeside or bowside and hence moving the rudder. The same principles of steering apply to the steersman as apply to the cox.

Turning the Boat

The cox should use the wind or stream to help turn the boat. When rowing against the stream and wishing to turn, the bows should be put into the fastest part of the stream; when rowing with the stream and wishing to turn, the bows should be taken out of the fastest part of the stream so that the stream is effectively used to push the stern around. When reversing the boat it is important to keep the rudder lines taut and the rudder straight. Boats should always be turned downstream of obstacles such as bridges or other moored boats. On many rivers, weirs may be another hazard and turning must be executed upstream and in keeping with the conditions.

Windy Conditions

When a cross-wind is present, the bows should be positioned so that they are pointed slightly into the wind (*see* Fig 132). Although this will cause the boat to move in a slightly crab-like way, it will effectively move the boat in a straight line. When the wind blows against the stream or tide, it will

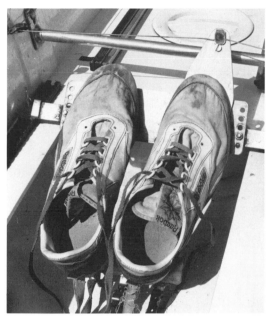

Fig 131   A steering foot.

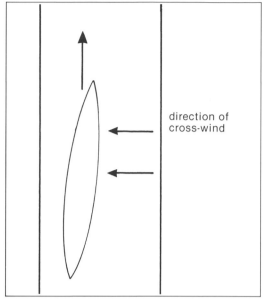

direction of
cross-wind

Fig 132   Steering with a strong
cross-wind.

slow down the surface water and cause rough conditions. On lakes this effect will become more marked the further the wind blows across its surface, and this must be taken into account during outings. On tidal waters, if the tide is likely to turn during the outing, originally calm water may change into very rough conditions and again this should be taken into account when planning outings.

Corners

When approaching a corner, the boat should move to the outside of the bend. The cox should steer towards the apex of the bend and allow the stream to push the boat across towards the far bank and out of the the corner. If going against the stream, however, there is a tendency for the bows to be continually pushed out, so the boat ends up at right angles to the bank — in this

case turning will require the stern to be brought out further towards the far bank than the bows.

Stake-Boat Starts

Many races start from stake-boats and it is important that the cox is able to get the crew on to the stake-boat without damage to equipment. If the racing is in the same direction as stream-flow then the crew should initially paddle quite far beyond the start to enable the crew to practise paddling with the stream. In order to attach the boat and crew to the stake-boat for the start, the boat should approach the stake-boat at a slight angle to the stream. As the rudder passes the stake-boat, the crew should stop the boat and then back the stern on to the stake-boat. This manoeuvre is considerably hampered by a cross-wind and, if possible, the cross-wind should be

Fig 133   A stake-boat start.

used to blow the boat on to the stake-boat.

When racing against the stream it is far easier to approach the stake-boat and attach the boat to it, but it is much more difficult to hold the boat straight than when racing with the stream-flow. The boat should be taken upstream and allowed to drift sternwards on to the stake-boat. Constant adjustments are needed to keep the boat straight, and in a very fast-flowing stream it may be necessary to hold the blades on the reverse feather.

Multi-lane racing is becoming increasingly popular and often takes place in calm conditions. The cox should initially line the boat up in the lane and then back it on to the stake-boat, keeping the rudder straight. The only difficulty which may arise is from cross-winds. Coastal rowing and many regattas have free starts — this can cause problems as the cox should try to ensure that the boat just finishes moving forward on to the line at the start rather than backing down from the line. Keeping the boat straight under these conditions is often difficult since there may be several minutes between lining up and the start. In a cross-wind or a current, the boat should be lined up at the extreme outside of the lane and the current or wind allowed to blow the boat gradually across so that major alterations to direction should not be necessary. If the boat is not straight at the start of a race then the cox must put his hand up to halt the start procedure. This must not be abused and hands must only be held up while boats are manoeuvring.

There are many situations in steering when the behaviour of the water needs to be understood. This applies to any rower or sculler and should be appreciated by anyone who goes out on to the water.

Changes in Stream Width

Where the width of a river channel narrows or becomes wider, there is a change in the

Fig 134　The 'hands up' signal indicates the boat is not ready to start
the race.

speed of the stream-flow, providing that the depth of the river does not significantly alter at the same time. If the channel becomes narrower then the speed of the current is increased and if the channel widens, the current speed is reduced. The stream is at its fastest on the outside of a bend since the water here has to travel a greater distance, compared to that flowing around the inside of a bend.

Bridges, Moored Boats and Other Obstructions

As a stream flows past an obstruction such as a bridge pier or even a moored barge, a low pressure area is created immediately downstream of that obstruction. As water always finds its own level, this 'hole' is filled with water downstream of the obstacle, which is moving against the general stream-flow (see Fig 138). This is an eddy current. The size of the eddy current is determined by the speed of the stream and

the size of the obstruction. Large eddy currents are caused by fast streams and large obstructions. Eddy currents and obstructions should always be given a wide berth.

Changes in Water Depth

When a stream accelerates over a drop from shallow to deep water a 'stopper' wave develops – this is particularly noticeable at the large drops found in weirs. A stopper is a vertical eddy current. As the water accelerates over the drop it does not simply stop at the surface level below the drop but continues to flow downstream with stream depth only gradually returning to its previous level. The 'hole' left immediately downstream of the drop is filled by water pouring back into it from the surface, creating a back tow which can be very dangerous near large weirs (see Fig 139).

A stopper wave is a major hazard if for any reason a boat or person goes over a

Fig 135   A buoy and moored boats cause eddy currents.

Fig 136   Eddy currents.

Fig 137   A bridge causes an obstruction, resulting in eddy currents.

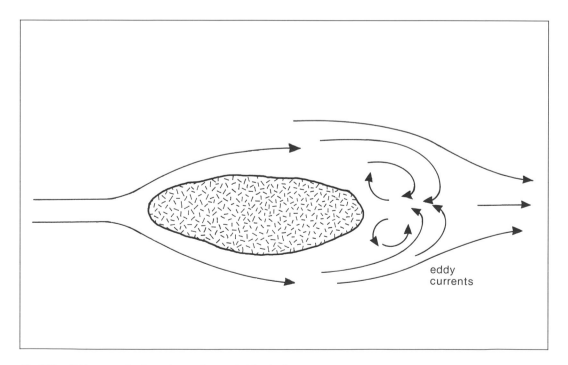

Fig 138   Eddy currents downstream from a bridge buttress.

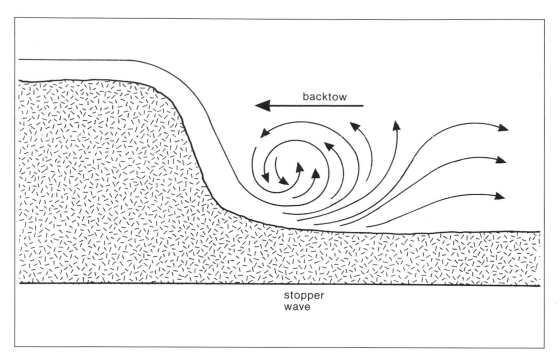

Fig 139   A stopper wave.

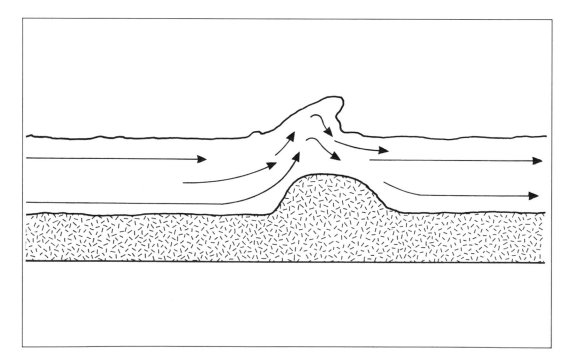

Fig 140   A standing wave.

Fig 141   Coxing commands.

weir. Any buoyant object failing to break through the stopper will be pushed down by water coming over the weir from above or may rise to the surface too close to the weir and be carried backwards by the back tow into the stopper wave. If this happens, the process will be repeated continually.

If the river bed becomes shallower the water will have to flow uphill and as it does this some water will break away from the general flow and 'fall' backwards, leading to the creation of a 'standing' wave (*see* Fig 140).

Wash from Vertical Walls

In docks and harbours, rowing often takes place in areas confined by high vertical walls. If there are coaching launches or other craft present which create a wash, these vertical walls can create problems by reflecting the wash back into the main body of water. This rebound wash can then react with the original wash from the craft to create very unstable water conditions. The interaction is such that at certain times the water may become calmer whilst at others it may become much rougher.

Fig 142   A coxing amplifier and stroke meter.

COXING COMMANDS

Exercise	Orders	Check
1. Taking the boat from the rack and out of the boathouse	Hands on − are you ready?	Cox positioned to see all of boat
	Lift	Lift is clean and not dragged
	Hold her strokeside (bowside)	Boat clear of other equipment
	Bowside (strokeside) under	Oarsmen are opposite riggers and opposite one another
	Half-turn (if necessary)	Riggers are clear of other craft
	Level	Crew in step and boat balanced
2. Turning the boat over	Strokeside (bowside) riggers coming up	Riggers are clear
	Turn	
3. Putting the boat on the water	Hold it strokeside/ (bowside)	Oarsmen duck under quickly and hold something substantial, for example, shoulder and not the slide runner or stretcher
	Under bowside (strokeside) Feel for the edge (of raft with toes)	
	Hands under hull	Oarsmen ensure boat is lifted well out, fin and rudder clear
	Keeping outside riggers clear of water − lower	Shoes out of the way and both level
		Bows face upstream
4. Getting waterborne	Inside oars in	Hands on either saxboard, same weight supported by each arm
	Hands across	

	One foot in	Foot nearest boat on to frontstop
	In	Other foot into clog and sit Blades in and gate locked
5. Checking crew readiness	Number off from bows when ready	Adjust to finish position
6. Paddling off	Come forward Light paddle Are you ready? Go	Check length of reach Ensure crew is ready
7a. Stopping (normal)	Easy all Drop	'Easy' as the blade goes in 'All' as they are extracted Lower blades on water
b. Stopping (emergency)	Hold her all Hold her hard	Blades flat and slapped on water Blades slapped, buried and held then reversed in water

Backing down

8. Varying the pressure	Next stroke Paddle light/firm Go	Called over three strokes Pressure change on fourth stroke
9. Turning Round	Turn bowside (strokeside) Go Change	Boat level Square blades Side called backs first Other side begins paddling
10. Spinning and alternate spin (faster)	Spin bowside (strokeside) Go	Boat level Whichever side is called backs down first, then the other side paddles on. This continues with each side alternating Blades slip across water
11. Manoeuvring bowside (strokeside)	Touch her (once, twice etc.) bowside (strokeside)	Needs will vary according to conditions

12. Manoeuvring sideways (used with strong cross-wind on stake-boat or when getting waterborne)	3 rows with 2's blade or 2 rows with bow's blade Go	
13. Rowing in rough conditions or wash	Next stroke feather high Go	Oar handle down and away to clear wash
14. Coming alongside	Strokeside (bowside) Feather high	Steer at an angle to stage Use outside blades to steer or hold Come in upstream/upwind Inside blades turned over
15. Getting out	Strokeside (bowside) out Bowside (strokeside) out	Side with oars ashore gets out first After all oars are out of swivels and gates are locked
16. Lifting out	Hands on, are you ready? Lift Hold her strokeside (bowside) Under bowside (strokeside)	Toes on edge One hand in and one under the hull Oarsmen hold something solid, for example, the shoulder Oarsmen move quickly and get opposite riggers

8   Simple Rigging

All the technical information given so far has assumed that the boat is correctly set up. The only adjustment that has been considered is ensuring the stretcher is in the right place to enable the blade or scull handles to finish in the correct position in relation to the body. At its simplest, rigging is the adjustment of the movable parts of the boat to enable the most effective harnessing of the athlete's power. As many boats will be used by a variety of people, a standard rig is most commonly used.

The purpose of this chapter is to highlight the adjustments that can be made to a boat, to explain the implications of these adjustments and to give broad guidelines to enable boats to be set up for individual crews. A well-rigged boat is important — athletes will adapt to a badly-rigged boat and will learn bad habits. Although a well-rigged boat will not win any races on its own, a badly-rigged boat will cause the crew to make technical errors and may even seriously impede the crew's efforts.

THE ADJUSTMENTS

There are five basic adjustments to consider when setting up a boat. These are:

1.   the stretcher position;
2.   the spread or span of the riggers;
3.   the overall oar length and outboard measurement;
4.   the height of the swivel above the seat;
5.   the pitch, both stern and lateral.

Not only does this list show the five basic adjustments, but it also indicates the order in which the adjustments are made. Most riggers have movable parts which are

Fig 143   *Steve Redgrave and Andy Holmes.*

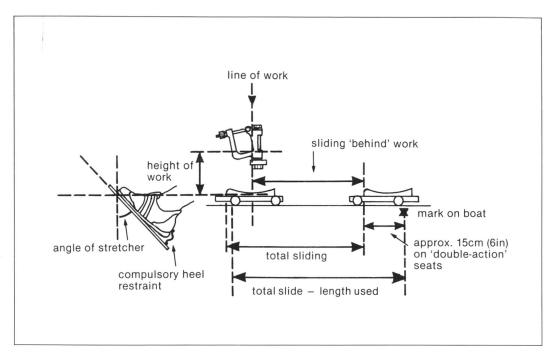

Fig 144   Basic rigging terms.

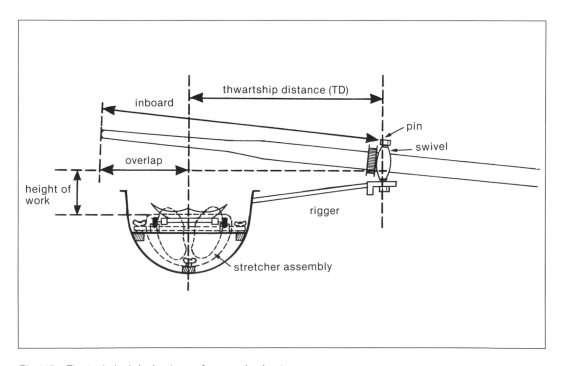

Fig 145   The technical rigging terms for a rowing boat.

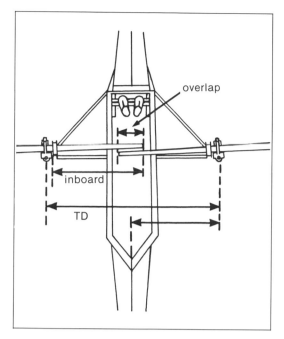

Fig 146 *The technical rigging terms for a sculling boat.*

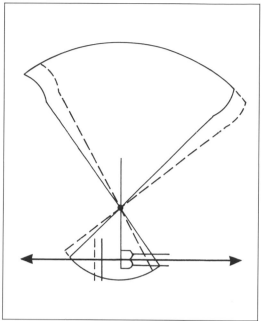

Fig 147 *The effect of adjusting the stretcher on the rowing arc.*

dependent upon one another and this is partly the reason for the order of adjustment.

Adjusting the Stretcher

The fore and aft directional adjustment of the stretcher has already been discussed in relation to both rowing and sculling (*see* Chapters 5 and 6). There are several other adjustments which can be made to the stretcher such as adjusting the height of the feet and even the angle of the stretcher (known as the rake). Although the fore and aft stretcher position should depend on the correct finishing position, the implications of adjusting the stretcher position on the arc of the stroke, should be understood.

Height of the Stretcher

The whole movement within the boat should be as horizontal as possible. On the whole,

boats tend to have large shoes to enable a variety of people to row within that boat. This means that people with small feet may have to row in shoes several sizes too big for them. This also applies to clogs. In recent years, to help overcome this problem, flexible shoes have been made so that they now attach to a plate which has a range of attachment holes drilled in it. This allows the rower to move his or her feet up or down. The balls of the feet should be set lower than the height of the seat. Since this up and down movement does not exist for clogs, people with small feet can overcome the size problem by wearing thick socks or even a pair of training shoes before putting their feet in the clogs. The problem that rowers should be aware of is the stretcher being too high whereby the reach forward will be restricted, or being too low so that there will be a tendency for the rower to overreach at the catch or drive upwards off the stretcher.

Rake of the Stretcher

The rake or angle of the stretcher is adjustable in many boats. For the average person an angle of about forty-five degrees is optimum. However, if the athlete has very inflexible ankles, or is lacking in height, the stretcher can be set flatter (in other words at a more acute angle) to allow a greater reach at the catch. The stretcher should never be flatter than forty degrees. The converse is also true − a very flexible athlete may be restricted in his or her forward reach by adjusting the stretcher to a steeper angle. If the rake of the stretcher is fixed, the feet can be moved up which will also restrict the forward reach of the athlete, however, this is biomechanically less efficient.

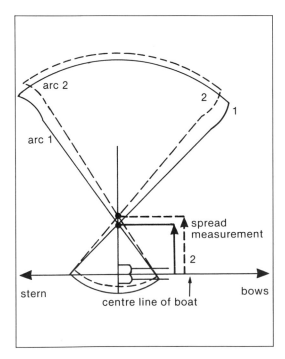

Fig 148   *The effect of moving the pin on the arc of the oar.*

Adjusting the Riggers

The rigger enables the apparent width of the boat to be small while allowing a mechanically efficient leverage system. The spread or span adjustments to the riggers determine the gearing ratio for a crew, and as the pin is moved away from the centre-line of the boat, the arc through which the blade travels during the stroke is reduced. As a rough guide, the smaller the arc, the less work is done per stroke.

As a general rule, the faster the boat, the larger the arc described by the oar or scull − this means that the spread or span will be smaller. Additionally, the faster the boat, the greater the distance the blade will travel before being buried in the water − a larger catch angle is therefore necessary. Also, the faster the boat, the less the apparent resistance is to an accelerating blade handle, therefore a greater arc may be worked through.

Measuring Spread

The spread is the distance from the pin to the centre-line of the boat. In order to measure the spread, a tape measure is required. Rowing boats vary in width throughout their length, from the bows to the 'fattest' point half-way down the boat and towards the stern where they are tapered. It is important when setting the spread to ensure that the distance from the pin to the centre-line of the boat is the same for each crew member. In order to make sure that this is the case, the width of the boat should be measured opposite the pin being checked (*see* Fig 148). The width measurement should then be halved and the tape held to indicate this value across the boat. The end of the tape should now be level with the centre-line of the boat and

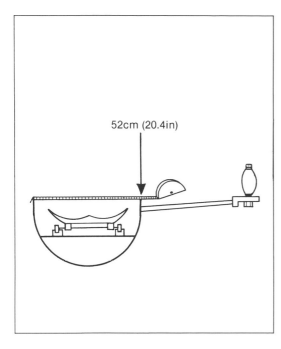

Fig 149 *How to measure the width of the boat.*

should be extended horizontally past the pin. The measurement is then taken to the centre of the base of the pin — this is the spread (*see* Fig 150).

Measuring Span (Fig 151)

In a sculling boat, the span is the distance between the centres of the bases of the pins. Since the sculler will wish to have both pins set at the same distance from the centre-line of the boat, it is important that each rigger is checked from this line as well as taking the overall measurement of the span.

Selecting the Oar

There are important standards that should be followed when adjusting or even

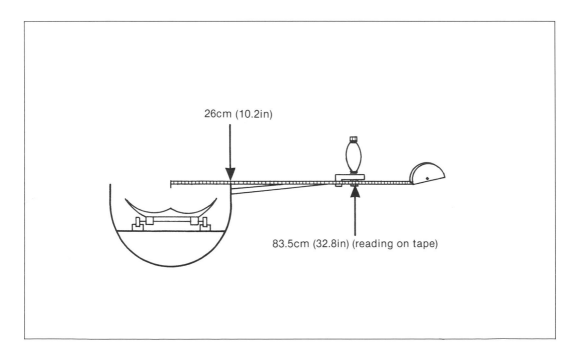

Fig 150 *The span is calculated by adding half the width of the boat to the distance from the point shown to the middle of the pin.*

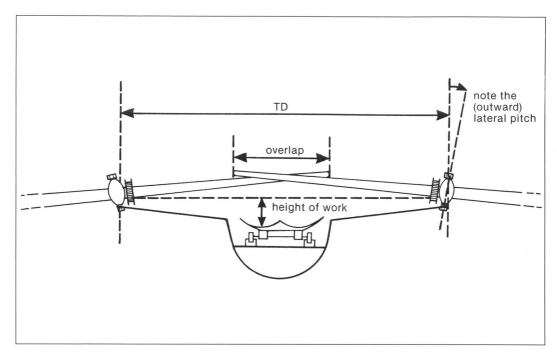

Fig 151   The TD and height of work measurements.

selecting the oars to be used in a boat. The inboard of the oar or scull has little effect on the feel of the work compared with the outboard length of oar and the spread. When rowing, the inboard length of the oar should be such as to give an overlap of 30 – 34cm (12 – 13in) beyond the centre-line of the boat – 32cm (12.5in) is the optimum. When sculling, the overlap should be 18 – 22cm (7 – 8.7in) with the optimum at 20cm (7.9in) – this is measured from the ends of the two sculls when they are held horizontally in the boat.

One very important point to note is that all rigging measurements concerned with inboards, oars and riggers should be taken from the centre-line of the pin. This means that adjustments need to be made for the width of the gate and the button, as a true indication of the outboard measurement of the oar will not be obtained by only measuring the inboard or outboard of the oars.

The overall oar length can be calculated using the following general formula:

The outboard measurement (from the collar) plus the spread (to the base of the pin) plus the overlap (32cm, 12.5in) minus the difference between the measurement of the outboard to the button and the spread to the centre of the pin (2cm, 0.8in).

The overall scull length can also be calculated using another general formula:

The outboard measurement plus half the span (from base of pin to base of pin) plus half the overlap (10cm, 3.9in) minus the difference between the measurement of the outboard to button and the span to the centre of the pin (2cm, 0.8in).

Boat	Rigging				Measurements			
	Span/spread		Scull/oar — overall		Outboard		Overlap	
	cm	(in)	cm	(in)	cm	(in)	cm	(in)
1×	158−162	(62.2−63.8)	296−300	(116.5−118.1)	208−210	(81.9−82.7)		
2×	156−160	(61.4−63.0)	298−300	(117.3−118.1)	208−212	(81.9−83.5)	18−22	(7.1−8.7)
4×	154−158	(60.6−62.2)	298−300	(117.3−118.1)	210−212	(82.7−83.5)		
2+	86−88	(33.9−34.6)			264−267	(103.9−105.1)		
2−	85−87	(33.5−34.3)			265−268	(104.3−105.5)		
4+	84−86	(33.0−33.9)	380−385	(149.6−151.6)	266−269	(104.7−105.9)	30−34	(11.8−13.4)
4−	83−86	(32.7−33.9)			267−269	(105.1−105.9)		
8+	83−85	(32.7−33.5)			267−270	(105.1−106.3)		

Scull blade size	Oar blade size
Length 48cm (18.9in)	Length 60cm (23.6in)
Width at tip 14cm (5.5in)	Width at tip 18cm (7.1in)
Max. width 18cm (7.1in) at 20cm (7.9in) from tip	Max. width 20−22cm (7.9−8.7in) at 20cm (7.9in) from tip

Fig 152   Suggested ranges of rigging measurements. **Note:** *the gearing is determined by the arc and level lengths, in other words the span/spread and outboard length; in general, the faster the boat the smaller the span/spread, so giving a larger arc in which to accelerate the oar to boat speed and thus enabling power to be applied to a moving boat.*

Fig 152 is relevant to men's senior heavyweight crews, but it can also be used to determine the required arc for other boats. The women's coxed four will travel at roughly the same speed as the men's heavyweight coxed pair and therefore the two boats should have a spread in the same range. Since the single sculling boat is for an individual this is probably the one boat where the rigging dimensions will stray most from the guidelines.

Adjusting the Height of the Work

The height of the work is the difference between the height of the sill of the swivel and the height of the seat. This distance accommodates the sitting height of the athlete and should enable the rower to be in a strong position during the finish of the stroke. Once the oar is at the finish, the blade must be extracted and sufficient room must be available so that the handle can be pushed down to enable the blade to clear the water. Not only must still conditions be considered, but the oars of the rower in the stern of the boat must also clear the puddles from the bow end and often the water may not be calm but popply. The rowers' hands should not collide with his thighs or the saxboard and there must be sufficient inboard height.

In rowing, the average height of work is 16cm (6.3in). However, there are some other considerations that need to be taken into account such as the overall weight of the crew, the size and design of the boat, the physique of individual athletes, the class of boat and the position of the rowers in the boat. If a crew is rowing in a boat which is too big for them, then the average height may need to be reduced and conversely, the height may need to be raised for a crew which is 'under-boated'.

In sculling, the two riggers should be set at the same height — the standard range is between 14 and 17cm (5.5in and 6.7in). The height for sculling boats in recent years has been raised as this enables a more horizontal draw together with better use of the shoulders on the finish of the stroke. As with the rowing boat, if the boat is too small then the riggers may need to be raised, or when 'over-boated', the riggers may need to be lowered. Many people rig sculling boats with the left-hand scull set slightly higher than the right. For most people, 0.5cm (0.2in) is a sufficient height difference between the two swivels. The reason for setting the left-hand scull slightly higher is because this is the hand which leads away and although it is in front of the right hand it is also slightly above it.

Measuring Height of Work

In order to measure the height of work, it is necessary to have a rigging stick or a straight-edged piece of wood and a measuring tape. The rigging stick should be placed across the boat on the saxboards and the swivel should be parallel to the sides of the boat. The seat should be moved under the rigging stick and a measurement taken from the lowest point of the seat to the bottom edge of the rigging stick (*see* Fig 153). Further measurements should then be taken from the bottom edge of the rigging stick to a position one third of the

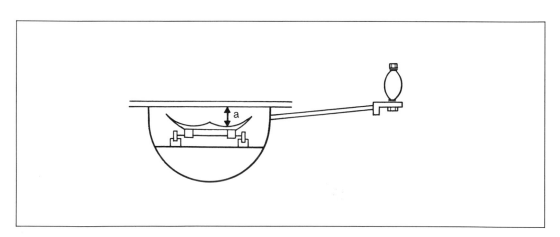

Fig 153   *The height of work is measured from the lowest point on the seat.*

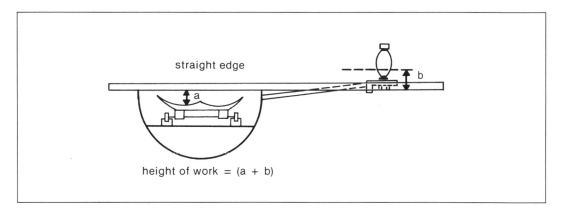

straight edge

height of work = (a + b)

Fig 154   The distance from the seat to the bottom of the straight edge is added to the distance from the bottom of the straight edge to the gate.

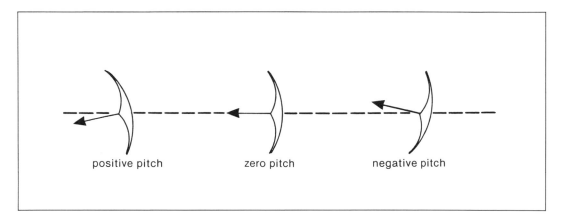

positive pitch   zero pitch   negative pitch

Fig 155   The effect of pitch on the blade relative to the water.

way up the swivel from the pin (*see* Fig 154). The two values should then be added together to give a height measurement. The rigging stick must not be measured twice.

Adjusting the Pitch

Throughout this book the emphasis has been on making every movement as horizontal as possible. However, it is necessary to put a slight pitch on the oar even though it would seem logical to keep the blade at a right angle to the water. The pitch tips the top end of the blade towards the stern. The reason for doing this is that however horizontal the oarsman may row, there is a small component of upwards lift as the blade goes into the water. If the blade is at right angles to the water it will tend to go very deep.

The pitch on the blade is a combination of pitch on the oar or scull and pitch on the swivel. The total pitch required is in the range of 4 – 8 degrees with an average of 6 degrees, and this is usually made up of a pitch of 2 degrees on the oar and a 4-degree pitch on the swivel. Most swivels are made with a built-in pitch of 4 degrees. In order for the pitch on the blade to remain constant throughout the stroke, it is important that

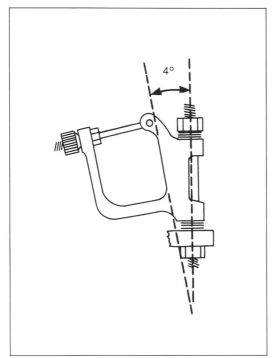

Fig 156   The pin is vertical and the swivel has a built-in pitch of 4 degrees.

Fig 157   Setting the pitch gauge to eliminate the tilt on the boat.

the pin remains upright and that any pitch adjustments are made on the swivel or the oar.

How to Measure Pitch

The most effective way of measuring pitch is with a pitch gauge (*see* Fig 157). The most common method used is to put the boat on the stools and the oar in the swivel with the measurement of the pitch on the blade being taken when it is in a position at 90 degrees to the boat and just buried in the water. The problem with this method is that it does not allow for any idiosyncrasies, and any variations on the pin, oar or swivel cannot easily be identified. Therefore, when setting up the boat it is far better to start by measuring the pitch on the pin which should

be set at zero degrees. Once this has been secured then the swivel should be replaced and the reading, and therefore pitch, should now be 4 degrees (*see* Fig 158). The pitch on the oar should be measured separately.

To measure the pitch on the pin, the pitch gauge should be placed with the measuring edge facing the bows on a level surface such as the inwhale. Most pitch gauges have a spirit level which enables any angle on the boat to be eliminated from the pitch calculation.

In order to measure the pitch on the oar, a flat surface should be found which can support the oar rigidly. The oar should be laid across the flat surface as if it were the face of the swivel. The pitch gauge, having been zeroed on the flat surface, should then

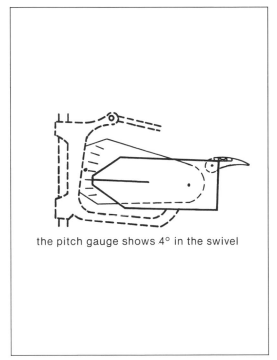

the pitch gauge shows 4° in the swivel

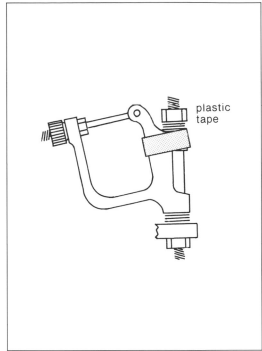

plastic
tape

Fig 158   Using the pitch gauge to measure the pitch on the swivel.

Fig 159   If the pitch needs to be adjusted, tape may be used.

be laid across the middle of the blade at its widest point and the pitch read off the gauge. Most blades will be set at a pitch of 2 degrees. However, it is possible for blades to be ordered with 0 degrees of pitch, but this tends to apply only to very proficient rowers.

Pitch Adjustment

If the pin is in the upright position and the angle between the pin and swivel is not 4 degrees the swivel may be worn and may need to be replaced. Minor adjustments in pitch may be made using tape on the gate (*see* Fig 159). For example, the blades may have 0 degrees of pitch but a pitch of 2 degrees is required. In this case electrical

tape can be wound around the top of the gate to increase the pitch. Likewise to decrease the pitch, the tape should be wound around the bottom of the gate. Some of the more modern swivels have interchangeable inserts at the face of the swivel which perform the same function as tape.

Lateral Pitch

Lateral pitch is the lean of the pin away from the centre-line of the boat. It is normally set in the range of 1 – 2 degrees and the effect it has on the stern pitch is to reduce it as the blade goes through the stroke. The importance of this is that stern pitch stops the blade from going deep at the catch.

However, it also makes the blade difficult to get out at the finish. By putting a little bit of lateral pitch on to the pin, the stern pitch on the blade at the finish is less than at the catch and this helps the clean extraction of the blade. It is very important that the pin never leans inwards. If this happens, insufficient pitch at the catch will cause the blades to dive and excessive pitch at the finish will make the extraction difficult and dirty.

RIGGING BOATS FOR YOUNG PEOPLE

Children should always be encouraged to scull, preferably in specially-built equipment, including the Playboats, the Tracer boats and even small-sized single sculling boats. The threshold level for young people using either specialist equipment or adult equipment appears to be at around a weight of 55kg (8st 7lb) or a height of 170cm (5ft 6in) — this is usually when teenagers reach fourteen years of age. The rigging table does accommodate people who fall into this category, however, for people below this age and size, equipment may need to be scaled down. Height of work and the length of the oar or scull will need to be reduced and the spread or span will be narrower.

Rigging is important not only for its contribution to boat speed, but also because if it is badly done it may cause serious damage. Technical faults will become apparent and inefficiency in power application will also be manifest.

9 Training

Usually people train with an end goal in sight and although touring rowing requires a certain level of fitness, most training is geared towards people who race. Technical proficiency is very important in rowing as well as the fitness component so it is difficult for a beginner to work hard in the early stages. As proficiency increases, so does fitness and there comes a stage when both work in the boat and on the land must become part of a set programme if races are to be successfully contested.

The rowing year is a cycle with different types of events and different training emphases in different periods of the cycle. The main regatta season for both coastal and river boats is from May to September; however, there are also long distance races during the winter months. The winter months from October to April are the preparation period divided into general and specific preparation periods, when the main emphasis should be on developing endurance, flexibility, conditioning and strength. As May to September is the competition period, the main emphasis is on developing a race plan, speed and maintaining endurance. The transition period between competition and preparation is often ignored but should include the maintenance of basic fitness together with a review of the previous year and formulation of the programme for the new season.

All rowing training is divided into bands that promote a certain physiological response and are distinguished for the individual by a range of heart rates. The training bands are divided into two: the aerobic energy systems and the anaerobic systems. The term aerobic means with oxygen and the aerobic energy systems are those that utilize fatty acids or glycogen as the main fuel source together with oxygen. The term anaerobic means without oxygen and the major anaerobic energy system uses stored glycogen without oxygen and so produces lactic acid.

PREPARATION PERIOD

Technique

Rowing requires the same action to be repeated over and over again, so it seems sensible to make this action as efficient as possible. The techniques for rowing and sculling and the principles involved in moving the boat have already been outlined. Although technique should be uppermost in the crew members' minds during all training, it is easier for major changes to be made during the long low-rating work which comprises winter training. If technique is to become consistent and effective, particular attention must be paid to the rower's technique when he or she is tired.

Endurance

As most races are in excess of 500m (547yds) they all have an endurance component. Endurance training can be separated into three types and they are:

Fig 160   *Beryl Crockford with a snatch.*

utilization (UT), transport (TR) and anaerobic threshold (AT). Utilization training causes an increase in the number of capillaries around the muscle fibre together with a rise in the potential of the muscle cell to use oxygen, thus enabling the muscle to work harder before lactic acid is created. In order for this change to be brought about in the muscle the training must be in the range of 65 – 85 per cent of the individual's maximum heart rate. This requires low-intensity work for long periods of time. Transport training improves the heart and lungs' ability to provide oxygen-rich blood to the muscles. The pulse range for this type of training is 85 95 per cent of the individual's maximum heart rate. In order to work at this heart rate, fairly intensive pieces of work need to be undertaken.

Anaerobic threshold training is attempting to raise the heart rate at which the body moves from using only oxygen to using oxygen and producing lactic acid. This training range is at 80 – 90 per cent of the individual's heart rate or, if known, at or just below their anaerobic threshold.

All endurance training can be undertaken in the boat or by cycling, swimming, running or using an ergometer. A variety of training activities is important in the winter months when the content of the training sessions is often similar. There is also the possibility of losing water sessions because of adverse weather and these will need to be completed through another activity that is already appearing in the training programme.

Strength

The rower has to lever both the weight of the boat and the people in it past the blades. Thus, the greater the strength of the rower, the quicker the acceleration of the oar handle and the faster the boat will go. Strength training is carried out on land using resistance either in the form of bodyweight or weights such as dumb-bells and barbells. It is also possible for a rower to develop strength in the boat or on the ergometer by practising low-rating short bursts with the aim of moving the boat as far as possible with each stroke. This form of training is normally developed during the preparation period. A word of caution: strength training should not be undertaken by pre-pubescent youths.

COMPETITION PERIOD

Technique and endurance training are still the main components of training during the

Fig 161 *Cycling improves general endurance.*

competition period. However, the anaerobic system must also be developed through training. Training at heart rates in excess of 95 per cent of an individual's maximum heart rate will improve the anaerobic energy system in two ways: the first is to increase the enzymes that enable glycogen to be used as a fuel by the muscles without the presence of oxygen, and the second is an increase in the body's ability to withstand lactic acid. These two effects are brought about by training for lactic acid tolerance (LT) or production (LP). There is a third type of anaerobic energy system which uses the chemical bonds already stored in the muscle fibre. This energy source does not produce lactic acid but is only available for a very small part of any rowing race and so is not usually

Fig 162 *Strength training — the power clean position.*

Fig 163 *The high pull with weights.*

trained specifically; however, practising starts will train this energy source.

TRANSITION PERIOD

The transition period is usually one month long and is sandwiched between the competition and preparation periods. This time should be used to review the previous season and then use the information to plan the following year. An important aspect of this period is for the rower to continue with some aerobic activity to maintain a basic level of fitness. However, this should be different from the type of activities usually included in the training schedule.

PLANNING THE YEAR

Before any training starts it is important to plan the whole year, and since most people train to race then the main aim of the season will determine the outline of the year's programme. The main aim or goal of the season should be entered as the final race of the competition period and the year should be planned in cycles of four weeks leading up to this point. The start of the side-by-side racing season will determine the start of the competition period which is normally five months long. The start of the training year to the competition period is the preparation period divided into the general preparation period of three to four months and the specific preparation period of two to three months. The transition period links the two seasons together and should allow the body and mind to recover from the previous season while preparing to enter the new training year. Once the year is divided into four-weekly cycles then the balance of training required within each of these cycles must be considered together with the number of weekly training sessions. Apart from the main event aimed at for the season there may be other important events in the timetable. These should be placed at the end of a four-weekly cycle allowing proper preparation for the event. Other events may be included elsewhere in the schedule but as part of the normal training programme and not given special preparation. This notion of four-weekly cycles and fitting races into this programme is important since there is a limit to the number of times a crew can peak in a season and still maintain boat speed. A crew that peaks to win at the beginning of the season is unlikely to maintain this form continuously to the end of the regatta season.

SUGGESTED TRAINING PROGRAMMES

The following information is intended to assist athletes in preparing a training programme linked to the competitive season. Since the amount of training and local conditions will in some way dictate the exact nature of the programme, the information only gives guidelines.

General Preparation Period (Months 1 – 2)

Aim To improve general endurance and technique on the water and general endurance and flexibility on the land with the introduction of strength training.

Balance 5 utilization/2 gym sessions.

Water (100 per cent endurance.) Utilization training.

Land (Flexibility, endurance and strength.) Running, cycling, swimming, ergometers, commando circuits, general endurance circuits, flexibility exercises and strength endurance.

General Preparation Period (Months 3−4)

Aim To improve endurance and technique on the water, and strength and flexibility on the land.

Balance 2 utilization/2 transport/3 gym sessions.

Water (100 per cent endurance.) Utilization and transport training.

Land (Flexibility, endurance and strength.) Running, cycling, swimming, ergometers, general endurance circuits, flexibility exercises, strength endurance, power and maximum strength.

Specific Preparation Period (Months 5−7)

Aim To improve the quality of endurance training and maintain strength.

Balance 1 utilization/4 transport/1 anaerobic threshold/2 gym sessions.

Water (100 per cent endurance.) Utilization, transport and anaerobic threshold training.

Land (Flexibility, endurance and strength.) Running, cycling, swimming, ergometers, flexibility, general endurance circuits, strength endurance circuits, power circuits and maximum strength.

Competition Period without race (Months 8−11)

Aim To improve the quality of the endurance training.

Balance 4 utilization/5 transport/1 anaerobic threshold.

Water (Mainly endurance.) Utilization, transport and anaerobic threshold training.

Land (Flexibility, strength.) Running, flexibility and strength endurance circuits.

Competition Period with race (Months 8−11)

Aim To improve lactate tolerance and decrease work intensity.

Balance 6 utilization/1 transport/1 lactate production/race.

Water (Mainly endurance.) Utilization, transport and lactate production.

THE VARIETY OF WATER TRAINING

The above section gives guidelines as to the training emphases at particular times of the year and also gives an indication of the balance between the different types of training. For example, at the beginning of the season all the training is utilization with some strength training. The variety of methods available for achieving a training effect are set out below.

All the training listed is based on the maximum heart rate of an individual being around 200 beats per minute. In order for this training to be effective it is very important for the heart rate to be monitored. A heart-rate monitor is the most effective method to measure heart rate but the pulse may also be counted by hand for a short time immediately after stopping work. This is reasonably accurate up to a heart rate of 180 but beyond this the inability of the rower to complete whole sentences while training indicates that this point has been passed.

All training must be progressive in order to enable the individual to improve performance. The general rule is that a hard day's training is followed by an easy day, but there must be a progression in training from one week to the next. This is reflected in the gradual transition from all utilization 2 training to include some utilization 1 and then a transfer to mainly transport training. As the season progresses so does the quality of the work.

UTILIZATION TRAINING

Utilization training may be divided into two types, 1 and 2: 1 has a heart range of 150−170 and 2 a heart range of 130−150. Utilization 2 training refers to continuous training in the boat for a period of twenty-five minutes up to 120 minutes with a rating of 18−22 strokes per minute. This type of training is used throughout the year and constitutes the main training form in the general preparation period. Utilization 2 is also used to precede most of the higher quality training sessions such as transport training and anaerobic training sessions.

Utilization 1 appears in the training programme during the specific preparation period and the competition period. The main difference is the quality of work and the higher or varied ratings of 18−34. An example of this variation is alternate training with five minutes at 22−24 followed by five minutes at 24−26 for a continuous period of 60−120 minutes. Another variation is to have bursts of 10−15 strokes every two to three minutes at a rating of 32−34 within a continuous sixty-minute piece of work at a rating of 18−24. This last variation will cause the heart rate to fluctuate between 130 and 180 beats per minute.

TRANSPORT TRAINING

Transport training is introduced into the programme in the late preparation period and then forms an increasing proportion of the training throughout the competition period. This method involves sets of work of three to ten minutes with active recovery in between. Often the work is broken into sections with the rate increasing at the start of each section.

ANAEROBIC TRAINING

This training is either carried out over a one hour period with an increase in rating each twenty minutes or as three intensive pieces of work ten to twelve minutes long with eight to ten minutes' rest.

LACTATE PRODUCTION

Lactate production requires the heart rate to be at maximum so the work is of short duration, up to three and a half minutes, but with a longer rest to work ratio to allow for the removal of as much lactate as possible.

Each period of the year is covered in the

above list, which highlights the nature of the work required and the percentage of the overall session to be spent on each activity. As long as the various aspects of training are kept in the correct proportions then the aim of these training periods will be met and the athlete will be ready to race during the competitive season.

THE VARIETY OF LAND TRAINING

In the winter many people find it difficult to get on the water during the week so they train on land. The running, cycling, swimming and ergometer activities are mainly used for improving general endurance. The ergometer (*see* Figs 164 and 165) is an important tool for monitoring consistency during training. All these activities can be used for any of the types of training already listed as water work.

Flexibility

In order to perform any sport it is important that the athlete is flexible with a greater range of movement than is necessary to perform that activity. During the early part of the season it is important that time is spent in developing flexibility, especially before any weight training is undertaken.

Commando Circuits
(*Fig 168*)

These circuits are continuous, low-quality endurance activities. The sorts of activity that may be included are jumping over and crawling under boxes, shuttle runs or any other activity which keeps the athlete on the move. This type of training is usually carried out at the beginning of the season to develop general endurance. The duration can be built up gradually from ten minutes to an hour of continuous activity.

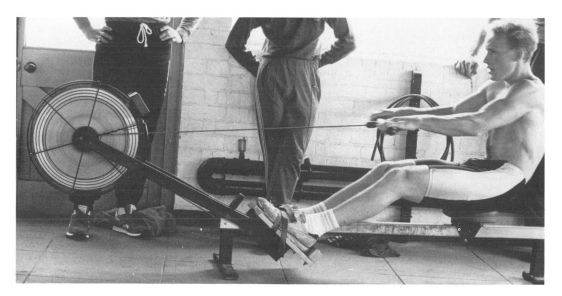

Fig 164 and 165   The ergometer which can be used to improve general endurance.

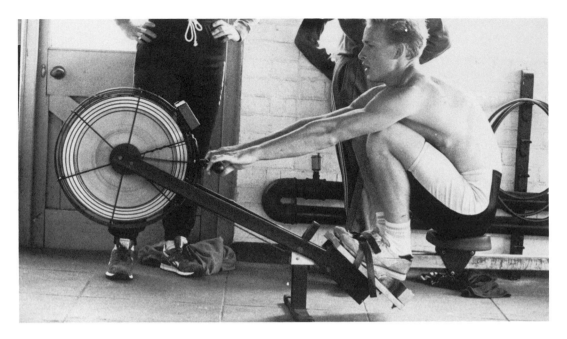

Fig 165

General Endurance Circuits

This circuit can be carried out anywhere and virtually no equipment is required. It serves the same purpose as the commando circuit but relies on activities such as squat jumps, sit-ups or any other activity which can be carried out at a rate of between forty and sixty repetitions per minute. The idea of this circuit is to produce continuous movement and the duration can be built up gradually from ten minutes to an hour. For examples of exercise, *see* Figs 169 – 79.

STRENGTH ENDURANCE CIRCUITS

Strength endurance circuits are intended to strengthen the whole body of the athlete rather than concentrating on the particular muscle groups used within the sport. Strength circuits are usually carried out using resistance in the form of body weight or weights such as dumb-bells and barbells.

POWER TRAINING

Power training will build the necessary power in the muscles used in executing the rowing action. It is important for the rower to be able to produce the power in order to accelerate the blade handle, and so strength training is an important part of winter training. Youngsters should rely upon body weight or light weights as the only resistance for this type of training.

shoulder mobility exercises

trunk rotation

back mobility exercises

quadriceps stretch

trunk side flexion

hip mobility

Fig 166 Flexibility circuit 1.

hamstring and abductor stretch

trunk stretch

leg abductor stretch

hamstring stretch

gastrocnemius stretch

quadriceps stretch

soleus stretch

Fig 167 Flexibility circuit 2.

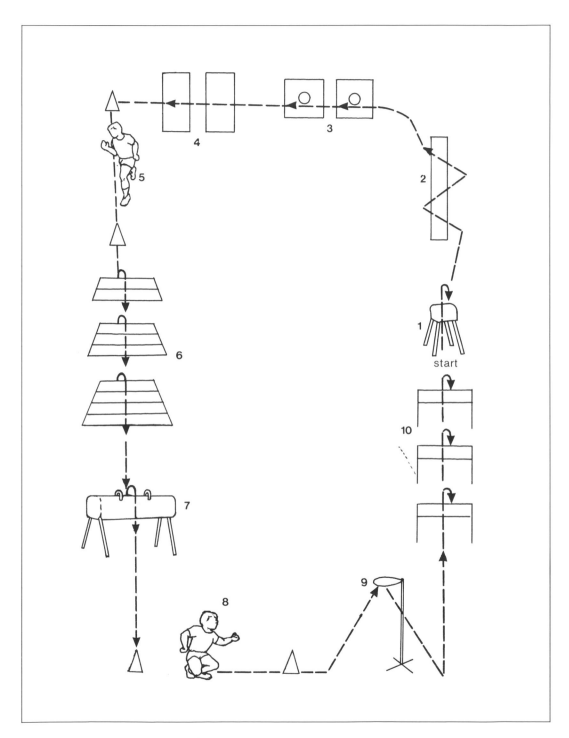

Fig 168   An example of a commando
circuit.

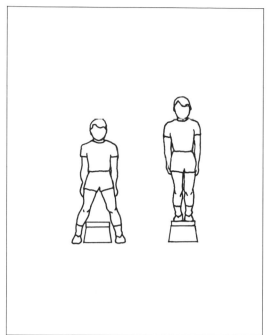

Fig 169   Box astride jumps.

Fig 170   Dorsal rise.

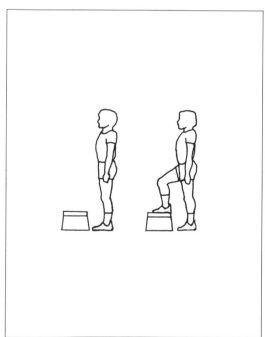

Fig 171   Step-ups.

Fig 172   Burpees.

Fig 173   Squat jumps.

Fig 174   Sit-ups — always with bent knees.

Fig 175   Variations of press-ups.

Fig 176   Shuttle runs.

Fig 177   Burpees and jumps.

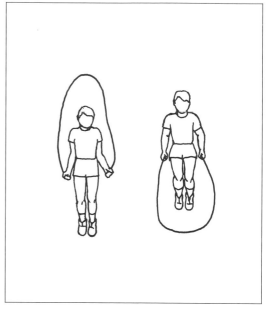

Fig 178   Skipping.

Fig 179   Side to side bench jumps.

MAXIMUM STRENGTH TRAINING

Maximum strength training should only be undertaken by athletes with a good general strength base. This activity concentrates on five lifts specific to the rowing stroke: half squat, sit up, dorsal rise, power clean and bench pull. This type of training should be carefully monitored and safety should always be of prime importance.

EFFECTS OF TRAINING ON THE BODY

All too often, little explanation is given as to why an athlete is performing a particular mode of training. This may lead to the athlete changing the session or cutting the rest period short in the mistaken belief that more must produce a better result. If this happens, the chances are that the very

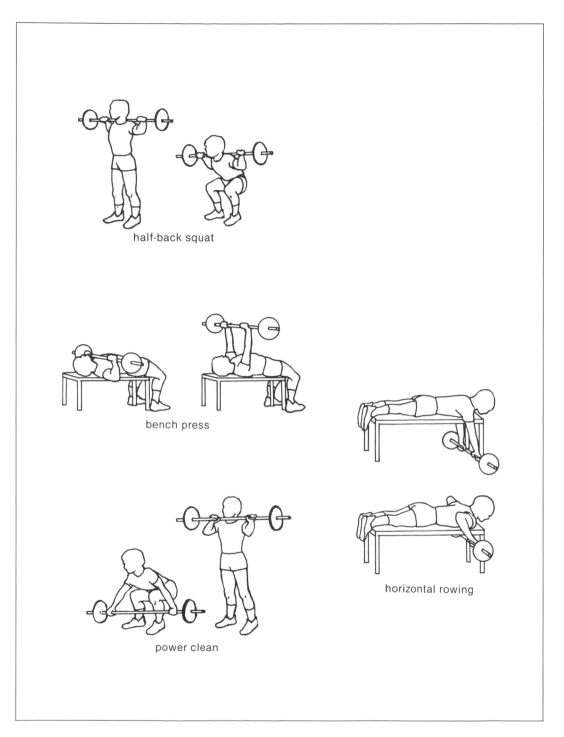

half-back squat

bench press

horizontal rowing

power clean

Fig 180 Example of a strength circuit.

nature of the training will change and the balance of the training programme will totally alter. As already explained training attempts to bring about a physiological response in the body to make the rower a more efficient machine.

The first changes brought about in the body are the increased capillaries in the muscle fibre and an ability of the cell to utilize oxygen, the free fatty acids and glycogen more efficiently. The second changes through training are to the heart and lungs. The heart is a pump made from muscle which becomes stronger through training. This means that the heart can push more blood around the body, which causes the pulse rate to drop. A fit person can therefore pump more blood around his body at a lower heartbeat rate than an unfit person. This gives greater potential for more oxygen to be moved around the system during maximal activity and equally importantly the waste products carbon dioxide and water can be removed more efficiently.

The next major change brought about in the body is the increased ability to convert potential energy stores into available energy. The main energy stores are carbohydrate, fat and protein. Protein is only used as an energy supply in the absence of the other two stores. Carbohydrate is only present in the body as an energy source and has the advantage of being able to generate high rates of energy even when the oxygen supply is insufficient (through anaerobic respiration). Carbohydrate is stored as glycogen in the muscles and liver where it can be converted into glucose and used to supplement the muscle's stores.

Glucose is converted into a usable energy form by mitochondria which are present in all cells, including the muscle cells. Glucose together with oxygen are required for the process to take place and carbon dioxide and water are the waste products. Most oxygen taken into the body is used by the mitochondria. This process is mentioned because the athlete should be aware that during training it is possible to increase the number of mitochondria present in the muscle — an obvious advantage if they produce energy for the muscle. Also the food eaten is important and should be considered — a lack of carbohydrate in the body will lead to a lack of easily available fuel for energy supply.

Another important change brought about by training is that the nerve fibres become better at recruiting muscle fibres to assist in performing an activity. The more muscle fibres recruited, the better the power output of the muscle. Resistance training affects this process the most. Nerve fibres also become quicker at transferring the message, so that the reaction time of the muscle fibres becomes quicker.

EATING FOR TRAINING

Fat has not yet been mentioned as a viable energy source for rowing. Fat as a fuel enables the body to work for a long period but at a fairly low rate. Improving the fat utilisation of the body has little practical use for the rower since this only prolongs the period of exercise and does not increase speed. The body stores enough glycogen for two to three hours of continuous exercise, thus making fat an inefficient fuel source for most rowing purposes.

Carbohydrate is found in foods such as bread, potatoes, pasta and rice and also in refined products such as cakes, confectionery and soft drinks. The first group mentioned consists of so-called complex carbohydrates which have been found to be the most useful fuel for the muscles. The second group, or simple carbohydrates, are generally not stored as glycogen in the muscles. They tend to provide instant glucose which moves around the bloodstream. If a lot of simple carbohydrates are consumed, this can cause a release of insulin which eradicates the glucose in the bloodstream, resulting in a lower blood sugar level than was present before the confectionery was eaten.

During heavy periods of exercise it is important that sufficient amounts of carbohyrdrate are eaten. There is quite a lot of evidence to show that if muscles are worked on a daily basis without the glycogen being fully replaced, then there will be a decrease in performance fairly quickly. Initially, complex carbohydrates should be eaten, but since these tend to be fairly bulky and bland, some may be taken in the form of simple carbohydrates.

HYDRATION

Another factor which is very important to all athletes is the amount of fluid they drink. During periods of exericse the body loses fairly large quantities of water through sweat — this is the body's cooling mechanism. Research has shown that a fluid loss corresponding to as little as two per cent of body-weight can seriously impair the capacity of the athlete to perform muscular work. Even in temperate climates there may be a reduction of between one to five per cent of body-weight during prolonged exercise. In extreme conditions this may even be elevated to eight to ten per cent of body-weight.

Fluid replacement is necessary during exercise as well as after exercise. If the quality of work is to be maintained during a training session, then fluid replacement during exercise is important. Small quantities of fluid should be taken frequently rather than large quantities infrequently. During exercise fluid should be taken in the form of a cold drink as these leave the stomach more rapidly than hot fluids. A slightly weak solution of a commercially available drink or a fruit squash will be absorbed into the intestine quicker than plain water. Athletes should avoid the commercially available drinks which are highly concentrated, as these may slow down the rate of fluid absorption.

After exercise, fluid intake should start immediately to ensure total rehydration of the body. Alcohol should be avoided as part of this process as it is a diuretic and will cause further dehydration of the body.

10 Types of Rowing

Throughout this book, reference has been made to a variety of rowing opportunities which are available in slightly different forms depending on the location. The Amateur Rowing Association provides details of clubs, regattas and schemes around the country and local authorities should also be able to give details of rowing clubs in their area.

RACING

The rowing year is divided into summer regattas and head of the river races in the winter. Summer regattas vary slightly in distance from 500m (547yds) to 2,000m (2,187yds) with some involving boats racing side by side and other events being multi-lane.

The head races were originally started to test the training progress of crews during the winter period. There now exists a very comprehensive series of heads which enable boats to race nearly every weekend of the year. The head races are processional — this means that one crew at a time passes over the start line with a time gap between crews. The winners are decided by the crew that has covered the distance

Fig 181 Gig racing.

Fig 182   Racing at Henley.

between the start line and the finish line in the shortest time. The head races vary considerably in length from 1,500m (1,640yds) to 7,000m (7,655yds). Both the head races and the regattas cater for all types of boat, although the heads tend to specialise with either many small boats or eight and four-boat heads.

Most rowing clubs and schools regularly take part in regattas at various venues around the country. The racing structure consists of various rowing statuses which allow people to compete at their own level. On first entering the sport, the competitor is classed as a novice which means that he only competes against other novices. A novice is a rower or sculler who has never won an open regatta – once this is achieved the competitor moves up to 'senior 3' status.

Progression is then based on a points system until, having achieved twelve points, the person becomes an 'elite'.

Unlike many other sports this means that at every level the competition is against people with a similar rowing background. There are also junior events which are classed in age categories. At the youngest levels – under-12 (J12) and under-14 (J14) – the main emphasis is on sculling boats, both singles and crew boats. In older age categories the boats mirror those used by the adults.

Many regattas are now held as two-day events, either at one venue or when clubs join forces. Consequently during the summer period, many clubs go *en masse* to a regatta venue and spend the entire weekend rowing; this makes the sport very sociable.

COASTAL ROWING

The main venues for coastal rowing in England are along the South Coast from

Kent to Cornwall. There are also small pockets of rowing along the Welsh coastline and in the extreme north east of the country. In Devon and Cornwall gig racing also takes place but this is in fixed-seat boats. Coastal rowing takes place during the summer months and although there is some training on the water in the winter months, this tends to be limited by both the venue and the weather conditions. Coastal rowing has a system of status events similar to racing events. However, there are a number of qualifying wins necessary to change status and the names of the statuses vary slightly from those on the river.

Coastal rowing takes place over courses which are 2,000m (2,187yds) long but which have a buoy turn in the middle of the race, meaning that the crew start and finish at the same point. The races are from free starts and often fourteen crews row abreast. There is an art to the buoy turn and valuable seconds may be gained if crews can line up on the right side of the buoy and minimise the turn-round time. The South Coast Division of the ARA runs its own coastal championships and in addition the different divisions have a league system. The organising committee of any regatta has to have a stand-by venue to ensure that the regatta goes ahead if either the wind direction or sea conditions are unfavourable.

TOURING ROWING

Touring rowing is well established on the Continent, but apart from *Three Men in a Boat* has not had much following in Britain to date. Many of the rivers and some of the canals in Britain are very suitable for touring rowing and it is possible to link up rivers by canals in circular tours. The good thing about touring rowing is that it enables people of a variety of ages and abilities to row together in a very sociable environment and is consequently very suitable for families. Many rowing clubs do organise the odd tour, often with the aim of raising money in mind, but the tendency is for more foreign crews to tour British waterways.

There are several commercial companies that hire boats suitable for touring rowing. Decisions then have to be made concerning route and accommodation. Some of the hired boats have canvas awnings which allow camping on board; alternatively camping in a tent is a possibility and many rowing clubs are also quite prepared to allow people to sleep in their clubhouses. There are many good pubs and hotels along most waterways and it is possible to have a luxury tour where only the rowing presents any hardship!

FUN REGATTAS

Playboats and other solid children's boats have already been discussed. Many local authorities run 'taster' schemes for youngsters and finish them with a Playboat (or similar boat type) regatta. The following list gives ideas of the type of activities that can be included in a fun regatta, or which may be tried out in a group.

Suggested Races for Fun Regattas

For each of the following events the buoys are spaced 12 – 15m (13.1 – 16.4yds) apart.

Slalom Relay (Fig 183)

This event involves three competitors per team. The first sculler sculls in and out of each buoy to the sixth buoy and returns the same way. He or she jumps out of the Playboat at the landing stage and hands over to the next person in the team. All three competitors complete the course once.

Changing Sculls (Fig 184)

This event involves two competitors per team. At the start of the race, one sculler gets into position in a Playboat by the sixth buoy. When the race starts the other sculler races out to his team-mate at the buoy. The two scullers then exchange their sculls. The sculler previously stationed at the sixth buoy sprints back to the landing stage to finish the race.

Standing Up (Fig 185)

This event is for one competitor per team. The competitors stand on frontstops and scull in lanes. The outward trip to the third buoy should be done with normal paddling and the return trip done by backing down.

Boat Changes (Fig 186)

This event is for two competitors per team. The first sculler sits in a Playboat next to the third buoy. The second sculler races to the third buoy and the two team-mates change over boats on the water, with the first sculler racing back to the finish line.

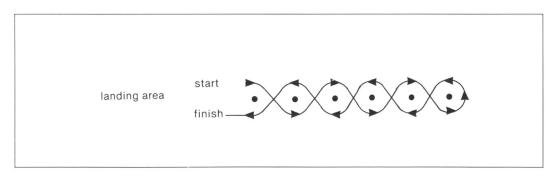

Fig 183   Slalom relay.

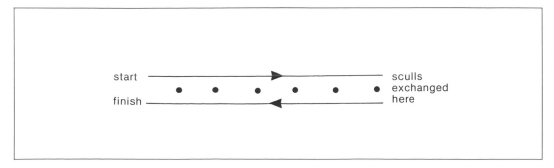

Fig 184   Changing sculls.

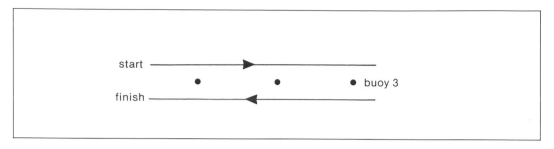

Fig 185   Standing up.

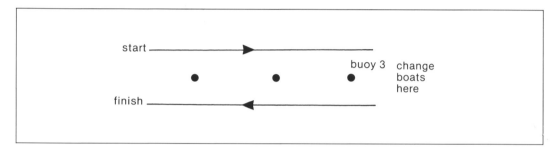

Fig 186   Boat changes.

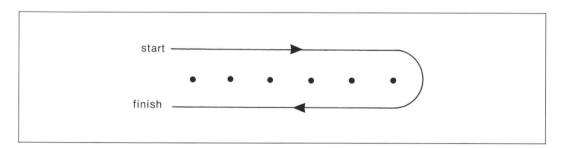

Fig 187   Forwards and blindfold.

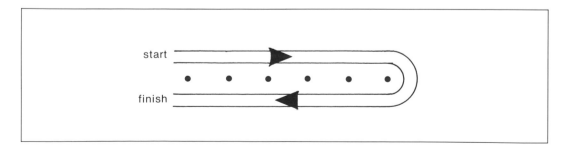

Fig 188   Sculling tandem.

Forwards and Blindfold (Fig 187)

This event involves two competitors per team in the same boat. The sculler is blindfolded and sculls to the buoy and back with the passenger giving directions.

Sculling Tandem (Fig 188)

This event involves two competitors per team using two Playboats. The scullers have only one strokeside and one bowside scull between them and scull to the sixth buoy and back, holding the two boats together.

The good thing about fun regattas is that rowers do not have to have any rowing experience as the nature of the events require skills other than purely sculling ability.

ROWING FOR PEOPLE WITH A DISABILITY

Prior to the 1980s, rowing for people with a disability in Great Britain was restricted to a few isolated instances of rowers and coxes who managed to participate in the existing club structure. Britain's first rowing club specifically for people with a disability was set up in Oxford in the spring of 1984 and the first disabled regatta was held on the Thames in late summer of that year. Since this time, the number of clubs catering for people with a disability has increased and several boats, specifically designed for this purpose, now reside in rowing clubs around the country. In 1988 Great Britain sent its first athletes to the World Rowing Championships for People with a Disability and the team returned with a gold medal.

This side of the sport is being developed and rowing can offer many disabled people a freedom unknown to them on land. People with a disability wishing to come into the sport should contact their local rowing club and although specialist equipment is sometimes required, much of the existing equipment can be adapted to accommodate most disabilities.

11 Proficiency Award Scheme

The Proficiency Award Scheme is a series of tests which allow individuals to judge their skill level or their endurance capacity. The award was originally set up for beginners and advanced rowers with different levels for participants to achieve. This award scheme presents another opportunity for the sport to move away from its élitist and racing mentality. The categories of award are watermanship, sculling, coxing and endurance.

THE WATERMANSHIP AWARD

The watermanship award is a prerequisite for both the sculling and coxing awards and it is recommended that it is taken before the endurance award. This award tests the sculler's ability to manoeuvre the boat in a totally safe and controlled manner and includes a swimming test and capsize drill. Once a sculler reaches this level of proficiency, he or she has demonstrated an ability to complete outings unaided. Scullers should, however, never go out in a single scull unaccompanied, no matter what their proficiency level is.

THE SCULLING AWARD

At this stage, candidates will already have demonstrated a proficiency in watermanship; the sculling award demonstrates a higher level of competence in a set number of moves. A holder of this award has achieved a high level of technical competence and has the basic skills in order to progress on to a proficient single sculling standard.

THE COXING AWARD

The candidates for the coxing award must have completed the watermanship award and therefore already have a sound knowledge of how a boat reacts. Within the coxing award, the cox must experience coxing at least two categories of boat. The concept of this award is for the cox to demonstrate a good knowledge of safety commands and watermanship together with a comprehensive understanding of local conditions.

THE ENDURANCE AWARD

There are three levels of endurance award: the 50km (31 miles), 250km (155 miles) and 500km (311miles). To qualify for any of these levels the rower must complete a set number of kilometres in a minimum of ten sessions or a maximum of ten weeks. The good thing about this award is that the rower can see the accumulation of kilometres through a series of outings.

Fig 189   The Proficiency Award Scheme
— a veteran crew.

Any of these awards can be examined by a holder of an ARA Coaching Award. A log book is provided and the relevant tasks or kilometres recorded. This scheme can provide good motivation for people who are just starting out in the sport of rowing or who enjoy recreational rowing rather than racing.

Glossary

ARA The Amateur Rowing Association – the parent body of English rowing, to which all clubs should be affiliated. All open regattas are governed by the rules laid down by the association and entries to these regattas are accepted only from affiliated clubs. The ARA promotes rowing development and also has a mandate to produce Great Britain's rowing teams.

Backstay A metal brace that usually attaches to the top of the pin to maintain the pitch.

Backstop The end of the slide nearest the bows. In bygone days when slides were short, a wooden block near the bows prevented the seat from running off the rails. With long slides, backstops tend to be the position the athlete reaches at the finish of the stroke when the legs are straight out.

Beginning The moment at which the blade is immersed and propulsive force applied to it. These two actions should be indistinguishable to the eye.

Blade The spoon end of the oar or scull. This term is sometimes used incorrectly to mean the oar or scull.

Blue A man or woman who has represented Oxford or Cambridge in one of the University boat races. A blue can only be worn by someone actually taking part in one of the representative races.

Bow The front or forward end of a boat. This also refers to the athlete sitting nearest the bow (also called the bowman).

Bowside When the crew is sitting in the boat, the blades on the left-hand side of the boat are on the bowside.

Bow ball This white ball is made of rubber or similar material, not less than 4cm (1.6in) in diameter and is attached to the bows of the boat.

Breakwater The V-shaped piece of wood or plastic positioned behind the bowman and separating the canvas from the stateroom. It acts as a barrier preventing any waves from entering the boat.

Button This is the plastic, circular collar which separates the loom from the handle and which is pressed against the swivel. The button is adjustable and may be moved to lengthen or shorten the inboard.

Canvas The material covering the bow and stern buoyancy chambers. This is also the distance from the bow ball to the breakwater.

Catch Another word for the beginning.

Clinker A method of constructing a boat's hull using overlapping planks. A boat built this way is heavier and slower than one with a shell construction but its life is much longer.

Clogs A wooden sole with a leather upper and a metal heel trap. This is attached to the stretcher bar – the athlete puts his feet into the clogs.

Cox A person who steers the boat by means of a rudder.

Crab This happens when the oar is caught deep in the water causing the athlete to have difficulty in extracting the blade. The oar may strike the rower or stop the boat.

Extraction The removal of the blade at the end of the stroke. The rower initially applies downward pressure with the outside hand and then rotates the handle with the inside hand to turn the blade on to the feather once it is clear of water.

Feather To turn the blade flat and parallel to the water on the forward swing. This must not be done before the blade is clear of the water.

Fin A piece of metal, plastic or wood attached to the underside of the boat. It provides directional stability by preventing the boat from slipping sideways.

Glossary

Finish This is the last part of the stroke cycle when the handle is drawn up to the chest. The hands must keep moving from the finish point to when the blade is extracted as the boat's maximum speed is reached shortly after and the water must not catch up with the blade.

Fixed seat The legs are straight, hence the seat does not move, so the rowing stroke is performed with the upper body only.

FISA The Fédération Internationale des Sociétés d'Aviron is the International Rowing Federation. It is responsible for the international rules of racing and the organisation of the annual World Championships.

Flexible shoes These are flexible-soled shoes which are attached to the stretcher bar where the balls of the feet are positioned and by a length of material connecting the heel to the bottom of the stretcher. The athlete places his feet in the shoes.

Frontstops The end of the slide nearest the stern. Sitting at frontstops means sitting with the seat at the front of the slide.

Gate The name for the metal bar which is tightened by a screw and which is used to close the swivel over the oar.

Gunwale The upper edge of a boat's side.

Heel restraint A length of material which connects the bottom of the stretcher to the heel of the flexible shoe. It stops the shoe from bending too far so that in the event of an emergency, the athlete can make a quick exit from the boat.

Heel traps The part of the clog that provides support for the heel and resists the downward pressure from the feet.

Height of work The distance from the lowest point of the seat when in the forward position, to the centre of the sill of the swivel.

Inboard The length of the oar from the handle to the centre of the swivel pin.

Keel The mid-line of the boat which is normally reinforced and around which the boat was traditionally built.

Lateral pitch The outward angle of inclination of the pin from the vertical.

Length This is normally taken to mean the length of stroke and is the apparent arc through which the blades pass during the stroke.

Loom The portion of the oar or scull between the blade and the handle.

Oar The lever used to propel a rowing boat.

Outboard The length of oar between the pin and the tip of the spoon.

Overlap The amount by which the scull handles overlap when held horizontally and at right angles to the boat. In the case of an oar this is the difference between the span and the inboard.

Pin The point on the boat where the force acts to propel the boat. Most rigging calculations are taken from this point.

Pitch The angle of inclination of the spoon from the vertical during the propulsive phase. It is governed by both stern and lateral pitch.

Playboat The funboat based on the BAT Canoe design.

Propulsive phase The part of the stroke cycle between the catch and the finish of the stroke when the blade is in the water.

Rake The angle of the stretcher from the horizontal. This is normally forty-five degrees.

Rate of striking This is also called the rating and is the number of strokes rowed in a minute.

Recovery phase The portion of the stroke cycle between the extraction and the catch when the blade is not in the water.

Rhythm The optimum ratio between the recovery phase and the propulsive phase. This may vary from crew to crew.

Riggers The metal outrigger supporting the pin and swivel. This effectively increases the width of the boat and enables the leverage produced by the oar or scull to be more efficient.

Glossary

Rigging The relationship between the inboard, the outboard, the pin position, the height of work and the position of the feet in the boat.

Saxboard The sides of a boat above the waterline which are strengthened to give rigidity to the boat. It is at the saxboard point that the riggers are attached to the boat, thus creating stress on the saxboard.

Scull A smaller version of the oar which is used to propel the sculling boat.

Shell Boats with a smooth, moulded skin of either wood or synthetic material.

Slide The runners on which the seat travels.

Span The distance between the centres of the bowside and strokeside pins on a sculling boat.

Spoon The end of the oar or scull which is placed in the water and which the boat moves past by leverage of the oar or scull.

Spread The distance from the centre of the boat to the centre of the pin.

Squaring Turning of the blade from the feather angle to an angle approximately ninety degrees to the water. This action is controlled by the inside wrist. The blade should be square before the athlete reaches the catch position.

Staggered seating Coastal boats are quite short, and in order to enable four people to sit in the stateroom, the seating is staggered.

Stake-boat A punt or similar smaller boat anchored to the river bed from which races are started. On modern, multi-lane courses starting pontoons are used instead which extend across the course.

Stateroom The area of the boat in which the athletes sit.

Status A handicap system which allows athletes of similar ability to race against each other; the coastal and river status systems are slightly different.

Stern The rear end of a boat.

Stern pitch The sternwards angle of inclination of the pin from the vertical.

Stretcher A metal or wooden bar across the boat which is secured to the keel and gunwale and to which are attached flexible shoes or clogs.

Stroke One stroke consists of a catch, propulsive phase, finish and recovery. The stroke also refers to the person who sits nearest the stern and who sets the rhythm of the crew.

Strokeside When the crew sits in the boat, the oars to the right are on the strokeside.

Swivel The U-shaped plastic mechanism which attaches the oar or scull to the rigger and which rotates with the oar or scull during the stroke.

Swivel pin The spindle on which the swivel rotates.

Thwartship distance The alternative name for spread or span, abbreviated to TD.

Timing This is when all the athletes move together in the boat in order to produce a synchronised stroke. Timing can also refer to the choice of optimum speed in order to catch the water and maximise the body's potential for accelerating the blade handle.

Tracer A class of single sculling boat with particular measurements. There are Tracer boat categories in racing and these boats are slightly more stable than shell sculling boats.

Washing out Allowing the blade to become uncovered (out of the water) during the propulsive phase of the stroke.

Watermanship This is the knowledge of boats and local water conditions together with the technical skills required to propel a boat.

Further Reading

Dick, F., *Training Theory* (BAAB, 1978).

Dodd, C., *Boating* (OUP, 1983)

Gill, C.J., *The Coxswain* (ARA, 1971)

Harre, D. (ed.), *Principles of Sport Training* (Sportverlag, Berlin, 1983).

Hochmuth, G., *Biomechanics for Athletic Movement* (Sportverlag, Berlin, 1984).

Matveyev, L., *Fundamentals of Sport Training* (Progress, 1977).

NCF Handbooks (National Coaching Foundation, 1986).
  'Coach at Work'.
  'Safety First for Coaches'.
  'Physiology and Performance'.

NCF Introductory Study Pack (National Coaching Foundation, 1984).
  Aldridge, J., Jones, H. and Pilgrim, N., 'Safety and Injury'.
  Gleeson, G., 'The Coach in Action'.
  Hardy, L. and Fazey, J. 'Mind over Matter'.
  Hazeldine, R., 'The Body in Action'.
  Lees, A. and Sheddon, J., 'Improving Technique'.
  Thorpe, R., 'Planning and Practice'.

Osborne, K., *Boat Racing in Britain 1715–1975* (ARA, 1975).

Ottaway, P.B. and Hargin, K., *Food for Sport* (Resource, 1985).

Page, J.H., *Learning to Row for Children* (ARA, 1977).

Sampson, A., *Winning Waters* (Robert Hale, 1986).

Scholich, M., *Circuit Training* (Sportverlag, Berlin, 1986).

Spracklen, M., *Hints for Steering the Coxless Boat* (ARA, 1978).

Vincett, R., *Know the Game Rowing* (EP Publishing Ltd./ARA, 1974).

Wootton, K., *Rigging* (ARA, 1985).

Wootton, S., *Nutrition for Sport* (Simon & Schuster, 1988).

Useful Addresses

Northern Rowing Council
Mrs G. Robertson (Secretary)
69 Salisbury Road
Newton Hall
Durham DH1 5PS

Yorkshire and Humberside Rowing Council
Mrs B.J. Edwards (Secretary)
4 Warren Avenue
Eldwick, Bingley
West Yorkshire BD16 3BZ

North West Rowing Council
Mrs J. Rafferty (Secretary)
276 Chester Road
Hartford, Northwich
Cheshire CW8 1QW

West of England ARA
Mr A.J. Jewell (Secretary)
46 Merton Park, Bideford
North Devon EX39 3AX

East Midlands Rowing Council
Mrs M. Marshall (Secretary)
60 Green Lane
Ockbrook, Derby
Derbyshire DE7 3SE

Eastern Rowing Council
Ms J. Botterill (Secretary)
32 Elstree Road
London N9 8QY

Thames Rowing Council DR
Mr B. Thorpe (Secretary)
149 Melrose Avenue
London NW2 4NA

Thames Rowing Council UR
Mr P. Blaseby (Secretary)
22 Bovingdon Heights
Marlow
Buckinghamshire SL7 2JS

South East Rowing Council
Mrs A. Salmon (Secretary)
2 Duke's Place Cottages
West Peckham
Maidstone
Kent ME18 5JH

Wessex Rowing Council
D. Drury (Secretary)
126 Sopwith Crescent
Canford Magna
Wimborne
Dorset

The Wilts., Avon, Glos. and Somerset
Rowing Council (WAGS)
S. Oxlade (Secretary)
92 Gambier Parry Gardens
Gloucester
Gloucestershire GL2 9RE

Coastal ARA
Mr P. Challen (Secretary)
92 Hoddern Avenue
Peacehaven, Newhaven
East Sussex BN9 7QU

Hants and Dorset ARA
Mr S. Bull (Secretary)
10 Brookfield Gardens
Binstead, Ryde
Isle of Wight PO33 3NP

Index

Index